THE NARCO-IMAGINARY

THE NARCO-IMAGINARY

Essays Under the Influence

RAMSEY SCOTT

UDP :: DOSSIER 2016

ISBN: 978-1-937027-44-5

DESIGN AND TYPESETTING: emdash and goodutopian

COVER PRINTING (OFFSET): Prestige Printing
COVER PRINTING (LETTERPRESS): Ugly Duckling Presse
BOOK PRINTING AND BINDING: McNaughton & Gunn

Distributed to the trade by SPD / Small Press Distribution:
1341 Seventh Street, Berkeley, CA 94710, spdbooks.org

Funding for this book was provided by generous grants from
the National Endowment for the Arts, the New York State
Council on the Arts, and the Department of Cultural Affairs
for New York City.

UGLY DUCKLING PRESSE
232 THIRD STREET #E-303
BROOKLYN, NY 11215
UGLYDUCKLINGPRESSE.ORG

PRINTED IN THE UNITED STATES OF AMERICA
FIRST EDITION | FIRST PRINTING

THE
NARCO-
IMAGINARY

CONTENTS

PROLOGUE

The narco-imaginary drifts throughout this collection. It supplies the haze from which these texts emerge and into which they fade.

Are these texts grouped together because they have been written "under the influence"? You can't answer that question with an unequivocal "no." At the same time, you are wary of answering at all.

You find yourself struggling against a warren of conventions and institutions—the partitioning of territory, at every conceivable level—not only the miserable American legacy of the division of lands, regions, and neighborhoods, but the regulation of discourse itself—historical and literary, popular and academic.

These pieces reflect your proclivity for the anarchic artifact, that which refuses the rules of engagement.

You want to say that you can be trusted, that you know what you're doing. At the same time, you want to say that *not knowing* what you're doing is crucial to what you're doing, crucial to what you have done.

Perhaps the concept of influence defines your province. You would like to suggest that what appears in this volume was written, in every case, under a variety of *influences*. Never one, always plural.

The influence of narcotics, the narcotic influence of texts. These essays broach matters that have altered your consciousness, both as reader and as writer.

You might be "the author," but you're not the authority. Before you say anything, why not dip into someone else's stash, sample the goods, take a taste.

Avital Ronell notes that Walter Benjamin begins his essay, "Hashish in Marseilles," with a quotation from Baudelaire's *Les Paradis artificiels.*

Les Paradis artificiels includes Baudelaire's translation of Thomas De Quincey's *Confessions of an English Opium-Eater.*

"To locate 'his' ownmost subjectivity," Ronell writes, "Thomas De Quincey cited Wordsworth."

No writing abstains; every text is written under the influence.

Language is the universal inebriant.

1

NOTES ON THE NARCO-IMAGINARY

The narco-imaginary, circa June 14th, 1966: Allen Ginsberg addresses the Judiciary Committee of the U.S. Senate regarding his experiences with psychotropic drugs. He explains his participation in Stanford University studies of LSD, and then he chronicles his own personal experiments with LSD. And with mescaline. And with ayahuasca. And with peyote—under the influence of which, Ginsberg notes, significant portions of "Howl" were composed.

Let Allen Ginsberg's congressional testimony stand as a signpost for the rugged, largely unmapped terrain of the narco-imaginary, in which the profile of the stoned artistic luminary and countercultural hero sparks and flickers amidst the gloomy atmosphere of mistrust and suspicion cast by the establishment. Thus Ginsberg, to the committee: "I hope that whatever prejudgement you may have of me or my bearded image, you can suspend so that we can talk together as fellow beings in the same room of now, trying to come to some harmony and peacefulness between us."[1]

References and rituals incorporating the hallucinogenic power of narcotics appear throughout the world's religious texts, from the mysterious soma that appears in the Vedas, to the tobacco, peyote, coca, and mushrooms used by native peoples throughout the Americas. In his forward to *The Greek Myths*, Robert Graves hypothesizes that, like its pre-Hellenic predecessors, Greek mythology is rooted in the ritualized use of *amanita muscaria*, a moderately poisonous, powerfully psychotropic toadstool native to most regions of the Northern Hemisphere, from Asia and Europe to North America. [2]

Heroic dose: the narco-imaginary establishes a circuit, maps an ancient course. The mystique that surrounds the narco-imaginary concerns its mythical beginnings; intoxication names the cipher through which mere mortals correspond with gods.

In his biography of Charles Olson, Tom Clark writes that, at the behest of Allen Ginsberg, Olson "drove to Cambridge, met with Harvard Psychology Department researchers Timothy Leary and Frank Barron at the Center for Personality Research, and was taken to the 'Mushroom House' in nearby Newton." After taking psilocybin, Olson described the experience as if "he had 'literally tak[en] a bite straight out of creation.'" [3]

"A bite straight out of creation": there is no beginning to the narco-imaginary, no point in time that can be marked as its origin. As Robert Graves would have it (after R. Gordon Wasson), the creation myths with which humans have for so long intoxicated themselves originate in the hallucinations of our ancient predecessors, reeling under the influence of psychotropic substances. The myth of creation is the creation of the narco-imaginary; the narco-imaginary creates the creators.

Poetic Dose (for Donald Allen): the recent history of the narco-imaginary is the history of postwar American poetry.

The pep pills that energize the amphetamine pleasures of the New York School, the psilocybin contents of the mushroom with which Charles Olson inaugurates his "Curriculum for the Soul," the heroic status of the heroin junky as conjured by William Burroughs—or, as described by Robert Duncan, the peyote-inspired work of Artaud that helped catalyze the collective imagination of the San Francisco Renaissance. In his essay, "Wallace Berman: Fashioning Spirit," Duncan writes of Artaud's *Journey to the Land of the Tarahumaras*—"opening the prospect of a Nature revealed anew by Kabbalah and by the drug peyote"—as a foundational text for the San Francisco underground of the 1950s. "A new generation was exploring the power of drugs to open up psychic depths and heights," Duncan recalls, "and the lore of drugs in religious ecstasies and in visionary flights of Romantic poets was the lore of the time."[4]

Reduced to its most common aspect, the narco-imaginary concerns the representation of drug use. The considerable pedigree of the narco-imaginary encompasses a vast assortment of cultural artifacts, religious myths, legends of creative reverie: the opium-laced visions of Coleridge and De Quincey, the mushroom-induced chants of María Sabina, Freud's cocaine dreams, Benjamin's experiments with hashish, Warhol's speed-driven Factory, Huxley's hallucinogenic visions, the LSD-inspired improvisations of Jimmy Hendrix.

Artaud in Mexico, seeking a peyote vision quest: the European colonization of the Americas stimulates a massive expansion of the narco-imaginary. And yet, if Robert Graves and R. Gordon Wasson are correct, such an expansion may represent a sort of return of the repressed; as European travelers develop an appetite for the psychotropic substances and narcotic rituals employed by Natives of this strange New World, their own bodies provide physiological evidence of pre-existent tastes, hard-wired hallucinogenic palates developed long ago, long forgotten.

Nonetheless, the narco-imaginary promises metamorphosis. In his discussion of Wallace Berman's artwork and methods, Robert Duncan suggests that Berman's use of "junk" is, in part, a rewriting of the narrative surrounding the use of heroin: "The word 'junk' that in the 1950s would have meant the trashing of the drug heroin, in the 1960s came to mean the redemption of trash in the recognition of devotional objects, emblems and signs rescued from the bottom in the art of a new context."[5]

The narco-imaginary, circa 1992: Kurt Cobain's dissonant guitar licks back William Burroughs' reading of his story, "The Priest They Called Him," originally published in *Exterminator!* (1973). It's Christmas eve, Burroughs tells us; to fund his next fix, a junky sells legs stuffed into a suitcase; dope in hand, he prepares the works, but cannot shoot up because of the moans that reach him from the room next door; he investigates, finds a Mexican boy undergoing a painful withdrawal, and gives his fix to the boy; returns to his room, lies down, dies—the "immaculate fix," as Burroughs says—and, "since he was himself a priest, there was no need to call one." Two years later, Cobain's body, discovered in his home in Seattle: fresh track marks on the arms, a bullet hole in the head, a shotgun across the chest.

Unmanageable dose: The potency and power of the narco-imaginary resides in its structural complexity as nexus and network; the narco-imaginary marks the intersections of healing and hedonism, heredity and happenstance, physics and politics, physicality and spirituality, phantasm and orgasm; the narco-imaginary is so real, it can only be imagined; the narco-imaginary may be demonized, digested, exploited, engineered, persecuted, prosecuted, celebrated, censored, marketed, marginalized, ignored, induced, targeted, tolerated, ritualized, rationalized, valorized, victimized—the narco-imaginary will never be controlled.

Though it may have no identifiable origin, the narco-imaginary nonetheless indicates the limits of the imagination. By claiming access to states of mind that cannot be reached without the supplemental help of certain chemicals, the narco-imaginary demands that distinctions be made; thus, even as its most famous adherents peddle fantasies, the narco-imaginary remains unequivocally rooted in reality.

The best illustration of the narco-imaginary as a failure of the imagination requires, at this point, an observation regarding Robert Graves' own narco-imaginary conception of religion as a product of *amanita muscaria*. Graves' theory is itself the product of a cultural and historical manifestation of the narco-imaginary, part of the mid-twentieth century fascination with hallucinogens as keys for unlocking religio-biological forms of ancient wisdom, as pathways to a mind-body continuum exiled by rationalism and ignored by Western science, banished by the Enlightenment and annihilated by Fascism. The mushroom coincides with a vision of the primitive, inviting users to imagine themselves participants in a primordial humanity that modernity seems to have forgotten. Here one finds Terence McKenna's stoned ape theory of evolution, according to which ingestion of the mushroom produces the great leap forward, leads humans into language itself, and for many thousands of years, plays a crucial role in the formation of an Edenic, orgiastic, hallucinogenic, ritualistic communalism, ostensibly ruined by climate changes that eliminate mushrooms from the African plains.

Dose of Reality: the narco-imaginary depends upon raw materials. Naturally, as might be expected, the narco-imaginary is substance-dependent.

Colonization reads as a diary of addiction fueled by the boundless desire of the narco-imaginary. Before the caffeine-driven exploits of the East India Company, consider, for example, the discovery of tobacco in the Americas. The tobacco plant serves as the cover illustration for Nicolás Monardes' *Joyfull Newes Out of the Newe Founde Worlde (part II)*, first published in Spain (1571), and translated into English in 1577. "According to Monardes, among the Indians not only did shamans use tobacco to conjure 'visions and illusions,' but laypeople also used it recreationally, 'for to make themselves drunk withal, and to see the visions.'"[6]

Ecological dose: the narco-imaginary is a biological, environmental, climactic, geographical phenomenon.

Amanita muscaria is native to most regions of the Northern Hemisphere, from Asia and Europe to North America; *cannabis*, Central and South Asia; the tobacco plant, *Nicotiana tabacum*, tropical and subtropical America. From the Europeans' first encounters with tobacco in the New World, to the Anglo-Chinese

Wars over the opium trade, to the more recent interventions of the United States in Vietnam, Laos, Afghanistan, Columbia, Panama, and Nicaragua, the chronicles of war and conflict are also chronicles of the narco-imaginary. The narco-imaginary fuels the economic, cultural, and political mechanizations necessary for massive mobilizations of people and resources. The creative reserve of the narco-imaginary underwrites propaganda and poetry, xenophobic panic and religious ritual, scientific research and organized crime. Rooted in and bounded by the same variations of terrain and climate that shape human populations, cultures, and conflicts, migrations of the narco-imaginary are marked by a history of violence.

In his introduction to María Sabina's *Selected Works* (2003), Jerome Rothenberg chronicles the events leading to Sabina's worldwide fame as a healer and shaman, and in so doing, provides a model for the trajectory of the narco-imaginary. Virtually unknown outside a collection of indigenous villages in a remote region of Mexico, Sabina and her mushroom-based rituals were "discovered" in the late 1950s by a series of American and European visitors, including R. Gordon Wasson. By the mid-60s, foreign visitors began arriving in waves, attracting government scrutiny and police harassment, and ultimately leading to Sabina's arrest and imprisonment. The seductive promise of the narco-imaginary invites state scrutiny; unsanctioned, the shamans of the narco-imaginary become the targets of state violence. The more the state seeks to control the narco-imaginary, the more the narco-imaginary asserts its primal hold over the minds of the people; state scrutiny legitimizes the power of the narco-imaginary to evade institutional oversight, regulation, and control.

Confessional dose: the narco-imaginary is a literary instrument.

Thomas De Quincey, opium-eater—and, consequently, explorer, colonialist, orientalist, literary experimentalist. Borne by intoxication, delirious embroideries festoon his narratives: here flies the flag of the narco-imaginary. Opium serves as his guide, ushering him toward authorial becoming; it provides entry into otherwise unattainable explorations of metaphor, pure digressions that delight in the possibilities of storytelling:

> Opium (like the bee, that extracts its materials indiscriminately from roses and from the soot of chimneys) can overrule all feelings into a compliance with the master key …. And sometimes in my attempts to steer homewards, upon nautical principles, by fixing my eye on the pole-star, and seeking ambitiously for a north-west passage, instead of circumnavigating all the capes and headlands I had doubled in my outward voyage, I came suddenly upon such knotty problems of alleys, such enigmatical entries, and such sphynx's riddles of streets without thoroughfares, as must, I conceive, baffle the audacity of porters, and confound the intellects of hackney-coachmen. I could almost have believed, at times, that I must be the first discoverer of some of these *terrae incognitae*, and doubted, whether they had yet been laid down in the modern charts of London. [7]

De Quincey's lessons on the linguistic possibilities fueled by personal experimentation with the narco-imaginary re-emerge in the innovative narratives that shape postwar American writing. William Burroughs' first book, *Junky* (1953), might be seen as one of the purest achievements of the narco-imaginary as a storytelling device; from beginning to end, the search for the next fix drives the plot. By the end of *Junky*, the narrator's drug addiction seems to be grafted onto language itself, grows its own sentences: "In another dream, I had a chlorophyll habit. Me and about five other chlorophyll addicts are waiting to score on the landing of a cheap Mexican hotel. We turn green and no one can kick a chlorophyll habit. One shot and you're hung for life. We are turning into plants."[8]

The publishing history of *Junky* traces the transformation of the narco-imaginary from a weapon of anti-drug paranoia to a marketable badge of countercultural authenticity. The 1953 Ace paperback edition, *Junkie*, published under the pen name "William Lee" and sandwiched back to back with another, now long forgotten book of pulp fiction, underwent a series of increasingly *literary* versions; as of 2003, readers can purchase the "definitive, 50th-anniversary edition" from Penguin, complete with a previously expurgated chapter, and an introduction by (as the back cover says) the "eminent Burroughs scholar," Oliver Harris.

Infant's dose: the narco-imaginary describes a longstanding human addiction to the very concept of beginning, what readers of Jacques Derrida learn to recognize as the fantasy of origins; the narco-imaginary is that habit of mind and body according to which humans dream the birth experience. To preserve the beginning, again and again, without end—and without beginning, because the narco-imaginary can only emerge as product: the narco-imaginary announces the failure of the imagination to imagine beginning.

The narco-imaginary, like any other aspect of culture, is gendered, classed, raced. *The House of Mirth* provides a primer. Though other pleasures escape her grasp, Lily Bart successfully romances cigarettes—in secluded settings, with select company, she freely violates the expectation that ladies of her class and status do not smoke. As with the immaculate fix that completes Burroughs' tale, the narco-imaginary supplies *The House of Mirth* with its ending. Before administering her own lethal dose, Lily worries about the "waning power of the chloral" that she has been using to help her sleep: "What if the effect of the drug should gradually fail, as all narcotics were said to fail? She remembered the chemist's warning about increasing the dose; and she had heard before of the capricious and incalculable action of the drug."[9]

Patriarchal dose: recall Flaubert's Monsieur Homais, disclosing the whereabouts of his arsenic supply in the presence of Emma Bovary; historically, it seems that women's access to the narco-imaginary has often depended upon the men who control the drug trade; a narco-patriarchy dominates the narco-imaginary.

In this context, suicide by overdose might be considered a revolutionary gesture: delivering her own final fix, the heroine short-circuits the power of the narco-patriarchy. Today, chloral hydrate—the sedative that kills Lily Bart, or that Lily Bart uses to kill herself—is rarely prescribed. Its use declined significantly after World War II, when barbiturates—which had been widely administered to U.S. soldiers during the war—became more common. Nonetheless, autopsies revealed significant traces of chloral hydrate in the bodies of Marilyn Monroe and Anna Nicole Smith.

Dose of fame: in the 20th century, celebrities preside over the narco-imaginary as the final fix for the unbearable pressures of public life.

Jacqueline Susann's novel *Valley of the Dolls* (1966), adapted into a film of the same name just a year later, popularizes the figure of the addict-celebrity as a dominant presence in the narco-imaginary. Under sway of the female addict-celebrity, the narco-imaginary courts tragedy, death, self-loathing—and, of course, fame. Street name "reds," "red devils," "red dillies," "red hearts"—and of course, as in Susann's novel, "dolls"—Secobarbital fixes Judy Garland, Tennessee Williams, Jimi Hendrix, Dinah Washington, Carole Landis, Beverly Kenney, Neal Cassidy.

Paranoid dose: in the media, the narco-imaginary provides a set of ready-made narratives, vehicles for fear-mongering, racism, police aggression, mass incarceration. The plagues and locusts of the 20th-century narco-imaginary: the marihuana epidemic, the heroin epidemic, the crack-cocaine epidemic, the methamphetamine epidemic. The drug epidemic is the fable by which Americans have repeatedly authorized governmental violence, racism, and oppression.

The narco-imaginary contributes to countless racial, ethnic, sexist, and classist stereotypes; enacted through legal means, the racist projections of the narco-imaginary scapegoat and criminalize entire communities. Thus, the notorious history of the Marihuana Tax Act of 1937, a piece of legislation drawing upon rampant racist sentiment sweeping across much of the West during a period of increased immigration from Mexico[10]—not to mention the notorious disparity between the sentences for those convicted of possessing crack cocaine, versus those convicted of possessing the same amount of powder cocaine (recently reduced from 100-to-1 to a supposedly more equitable 18-to-1).

Dose of revenge: the creative and cultural achievements associated with the use of psychotropic drugs provoke reactionary, sometimes violent responses by established authorities, institutions, and the state. Propaganda campaigns, stereotyping and racial profiling, anti-drug laws: if the concept of the narco-imaginary shelters the avant-garde's intoxication with intoxication, prints tickets to the underground, and preserves the right of the individual to remake experience as his alone, it also invites the paranoid minds of the pleasure police, the anti-poets, the modern-day Puritans, those whose desires can only be realized in the perverse enforcement of a fascist, equally imaginary, sobriety.

1971: John Sinclair, activist, poet, musician, founding member of the White Panthers, arrested for selling marijuana to an undercover agent. The agent, as it happens, has hounded Sinclair for months, repeatedly requesting that Sinclair supply him with large quantities of marijuana, despite the fact that Sinclair is neither a drug dealer, nor seems to know one. As news of his arrest spreads, activists gear up for his defense; a benefit is planned, Allen Ginsberg is involved, John Lennon and Yoko Ono want to perform, and the government discovers that it has supplied its domestic spies with a host of new targets, individuals provoked to participate in political activities following the arrest of John Sinclair.

Prison dose: the prison marks the intersection of narco-anxieties, the place where the paranoia of the persecuted addict meets the paranoia of the American public. In both cases, the prison validates all fears: as incubator for hopelessness, the prison confirms the addict's suspicions regarding the bankrupt so-called morality of his punitive culture; for the public, endlessly reproduced propaganda pieces masquerading as so-called news reports present the terrifying specter of a massive, frighteningly violent prison population of drug-dealing minorities and ne'er-do-wells. The solution: more police officers, more surveillance, and of course, more prisons.

In the process of planting, entrapping, or otherwise framing political activists on drug charges, the FBI's COINTELPRO tactics against the New Left reap the benefits of anti-drug propaganda, only to demonstrate, as if by accident, the viability of the prison system as a possible "solution" to much larger political problems, including problems posed by widespread unemployment and economic decay in the wake of deindustrialization. By selectively prosecuting drug use for political reasons, COINTELPRO begins a process that criminalizes the American Left under the auspices of anti-drug policy. As law enforcement agencies militarize their operations as part of the "War on Drugs," the prison regime effectively disenfranchises literally hundreds of thousands of political targets—potentially hostile minority voters, generally working class, from urban areas.[11]

Accidental dose: in its attempts to control, alter, or eliminate its appeal, the state validates the countercultural potential of the narco-imaginary.

That a propaganda film such as *Reefer Madness* (1936, rediscovered circa 1971) shall have justifiably achieved the status of cult classic attests to the inevitable limitations of the narco-imaginary in the hands of the inexperienced, the non-user, the uninitiated. Harry Anslinger, head of the Federal Bureau of Narcotics from 1930 to 1962, addressing Congress, circa 1937 (while advocating passage of the Marihuana Tax Act): "Marihuana is an addictive drug which produces in its users insanity, criminality, and death."

Legal dose: Charles Whitebread notes that in the years following Anslinger's outrageous claims, defense attorneys in at least five prominent murder trials claimed their clients suffered from "insanity" as a result of marijuana intoxication.

In 1948, Harry Anslinger appears before Congress once again to discuss marijuana use, now declaring that his agency requires additional funding to stamp out this growing threat to American sanity and sobriety. Americans, Anslinger says, are still smoking marijuana, perhaps in greater numbers than ever before. Which Americans? "Musicians," Anslinger claims. "And I don't mean good musicians, I mean jazz musicians."

Indeed, as Malcolm X chronicles in his autobiography, jazz musicians—including some of the greatest names in the history of American music—*were* smoking reefer. Malcolm knows, because he sells it to them. Even if he later espouses the Nation of Islam's party-line prohibition of drug use, Malcolm also understands that the story of redemption requires a story of sin; moreover, he understands that there is no anti-drug message. Every anti-drug message confirms the power and appeal of drugs as the gateway to a new consciousness—supposedly dangerous, apparently subversive, possibly revolutionary.

Dose of the Land: the egg in the frying pan ("this is your brain on drugs"). In the prohibition of drugs, the state commits to the sanctity of the narco-imaginary, acknowledges without reservation the revolutionary potential of the drug experience. No shaman but the state preserves the potency of the narco-imaginary.

NOTES

1. Allen Ginsberg, *Deliberate Prose: Selected Essays,* 1952-1995 (New York: Harper, 2000), 67-82.

2. Robert Graves, *The Greek Myths, Revised Edition,* 1960 (New York: Penguin, 1992), 9-10.

3. Tom Clark, *Charles Olson: The Allegory of a Poet's Life* (Berkeley: North Atlantic Books, 2000), 292.

4. Robert Duncan, *A Selected Prose,* ed. Robert J. Berholf (New York: New Directions, 1990), 198-9.

5. Ibid., 202.4

6. New York Public Library, "Dry Drunk: The Legacy of Tobacco in 17th- and 18th-century Europe," Sept. 20, 1997-January 3, 1998 (online archive accessed 9 September 2010: http://legacy.www.nypl.org/research/chss/ spe/art/print/exhibits/drydrunk/herbals.htm).

7. Thomas De Quincey, *Confessions of an English Opium-Eater,* 1822 (Oxford: Oxford UP, 1996), 48.

8. William Burroughs, *Junky,* 1953 (New York: Penguin, 1977), 147.

9. Edith Wharton, *The House of Mirth,* Scribner, 1905 (New York: Norton, 1990), 242.

10. As chronicled in Charles Whitebread's lecture for the California Judges Assocation, "The History of the Non-Medical Use of Drugs in the United States" (1995), the Marihuana Tax Act capitalized on the racism and fear gripping white residents of the Western states that shared the border with Mexico. For more than a decade, racist propaganda had promulgated fantasies of murderously violent marijuana-smoking Mexicans. (http:// www.druglibrary.org/schaffer/history/whiteb1.htm).

11. For a thorough treatment of this process, see Christian Parenti, *Lockdown America: Police and Prisons in the Age of Crisis* (London: Verso, 1999).

EVEN THE HARDY BOYS NEED FRIENDS: LETTERS ON BOREDOM

Dear Franklin W. Dixon,

Did Frank and Joe Hardy aspire to be professional athletes? I remember that Frank and Joe were whizzes when it came to football. I think one was a halfback and the other a quarterback. If they were so good in high school, don't you think they could have made it in college? I remember their father, Fenton Hardy (an intelligence man), used to trade clothes with the plumber so he wouldn't be trailed while leaving the house. Are all mysteries disguises for truths we'd rather not acknowledge?

My bloodshot eyes recall a latent criminality you'd surely recognize.

Ramsey

Dear Franklin W. Dixon,

My wife thinks I'm deluded. Don't you know, she says, Franklin W. Dixon's just a pen name. There never was anyone with such a name, and there were probably twenty people who wrote books under that name. Which one of you was really you? In one of your books, an illustration shows Frank and Joe astride a motorcycle. I can't recall who drives. Nancy Drew might be in these days, but doesn't that make you nostalgic for the days when boys could be boys? My brother and I used to climb on my father's motorcycle and pretend we were the Hardy boys. We sat in the driveway for hours. A friend asks if there was ever an erotic charge between us—he's perverse, my friend—and I'm left wondering whether it's Frank or Joe who was a scorpio.

Your glyptics produce heirlooms from trinkets.

Ramsey

Dear Franklin W. Dixon,

Did Frank and Joe Hardy ever get bored? I seem to remember that they always had plans, ambitions, organized activities: the big football game, the family vacation, the new hobby. Catalyzing abilities honed by the finest American upbringing, Frank and Joe fetishized squareness. Did Aunt Gertrude ever intrude on one of the boys masturbating to dirty magazines? She scowled and made mean pies, as I remember. On the verge of adolescence, I started reading the Hardy Boys. Late at night, my family asleep, I slipped out of bed to the bookcase and unloaded your volumes. This rediscovery—the books had been read to me, by my parents or my older brother, before I read them myself—made me a born-again Hardys fan. I remember the instant immediately preceding that critical action of rediscovery: summertime sleeplessness, the oscillating fan, the moon outside the window, the Oakland A's post-game show ending on the radio. I became static, immobilized by a desire so acute and non-specific that I could not move. Today I know boredom as this indeterminate, irrepressible desire that can't be satisfied by any ready-at-hand activities. At that time I didn't know Walter Benjamin's *Arcades Project*; I didn't know I was bored. "When we are bored," Benjamin writes, "we don't know what we are waiting for. That we do know, or think we know, is nearly always the expression of our superficiality or inattention. Boredom is the threshold to great deeds." I'm not vain enough to hope for great deeds; I'm waiting for your books to retake me, I'm waiting for Frank and Joe, I'm waiting for boredom. I think of Melville's Bartleby, whose answer to every inquiry is the same: "I'd prefer not to." Maybe boredom means to prefer not to—for every possible course of action.

Where essaying literature cools the hottest fires,

Ramsey

Dear Franklin W. Dixon,

I consider the phases of boredom multiple, as are its types, its durations, its synonyms: idleness, tedium, anomie...like the postman, chronic boredom arrives at noon. It lives in the basement, it emerges at predictable intervals, it never leaves the house; chronic boredom collects on the tops of shelved books, under couches, on television screens. Acute boredom is site specific. It arises in the midst of your subway ride, during a dinner with relatives, behind the customer service center at the bank, on the telephone; while you sit in the exam room, boredom appears on the poster showing various diseases of the digestive system. It abjures the open air, preferring instead venues for performance, movies and the theater, opera and the ballet. Boredom appears most brazenly in the teeth of the entertainer. Mr. Dixon, I can't help noticing that in your ciphered universe, every action betrays a sinister intent. Your villains thrust through boredom's half-drawn blinds. Framed by the window today: rain. A cold floor provides evidence, but I'm no detective. When every leaf tremored with divine presence, or so the story goes, no one went unfulfilled. I think of California, plate tectonics, the Hardys chasing drug smugglers in Barmet Bay. Tomorrow the kitchen sink, the recycling bin; I want to build a monument to inactivity, but I don't have the motivation. Let's consider your books paeans to madras. Let's consider drugs we've done when boredom strikes: amphetamines, marijuana, opium, flexoril, GHB, Xanax, LSD, Vicodin, Darvoset, tobacco, mescaline, Percoset, ecstasy, nitrous oxide, caffeine, codeine, Rohypnol, cocaine, psilocybin mushrooms, special k… When I say boredom, think "belligerence." In *The Twisted Claw*, Frank and Joe confront a wily crew of cold-hearted thieves linked to an international criminal syndicate. Did anyone ever tell you how much the Hardys' incessant interest and excitement, their do-gooder, never-ending, goddamn genuineness, wears thin? Sometimes their exclamations synthesize entirely diverse and universally repugnant elements of a generic American "Ah, shucks" attitude. "Oh, nuts!" Joe cries. "Whoa!" the Hardys' friend Chet exclaims. Today I read for single words: glockenspiel, gingham, galactagogue. I turn gaiety into galleon via Galahad; and while reading your books, I find sentences functioning as introductory passages for the uninitiated. Here's one example, the opening lines from *The Twisted Claw*: "'Congratulations!' Frank Hardy shouted to his brother Joe as the track meet ended. 'You've won the trophy for Bayport High and set a new record for the hundred-yard dash!'" Thanks to you, for a long time, I believed that narratives could only be written in past tense. Nonetheless, your name reminds me...the circumference of lawn sprinklers, the equatorial climate of the high school locker room...sense-memories glow at the borders of your prose, and for that I'm thankful.

From the basement, where dust glitters amidst potato crates and cracked picture frames,

Ramsey

Dear Franklin W. Dixon,

You may be right in thinking—as I know you do, because of the letter you haven't sent—that my project is corrupt, my methods suspect, my thesis nonexistent. What kind of ego-driven half-baked lit-crit is this? Arguments won't change your mind. Arguments lodge pigeons, decorate café walls, contribute to group neuroses. We're both interested in criminal mischief and difficult conundrums. We want truths to emerge in stages. I'm asking for you to believe me when I say there's no use cramming every correct quote into some damn essay. I'm suggesting that criticism open up to language, quit pretending anyone's in control. In these letters, wind enters unimpeded, architectural entrails provide diminished structure to damaged details, fabric and muscle merge, water spills amidst furnaces. I don't have a thesis because disjunctions between objects and images provide ample opportunity for the potential continuity of quasi-nocturnal memories, illuminations that fear the shadows of arches and borders. If you still don't understand my project, consider the continuing embarrassment caused by biological functions.

Yours,

Ramsey

Dear Franklin W. Dixon,

Lying on my back, I stare at paint cracks in the ceiling until my focus blurs and I see filaments drifting on the surface of my eyeball. Is boredom a drifting of attention, or a failure to drift? I won't detail the condensation of my apathy; I'm writing to you because letters pervert by degrees. Some commentators locate existentialism in the disparity between desire and self-censorship; for Kierkegaard, between temporal and eternal forms of existence, disparity opens onto three kinds of despair. I only have one kind, maybe two on my best days. Nonetheless, I can find disquiet in the finest filleted tilapia. Scaling a wall, Frank and Joe investigate strange noises coming from an abandoned mill. Your fascination with boys and their curious errands doesn't interest me as much as your refusal to let them stray into transgressive behaviors. Your characters are wax models for good objects; I want the melted version, the version that's been left out in the sun for too long.

Good luck with your hothouse for parted hair,

Ramsey

Dear Franklin W. Dixon,

Did Frank and Joe ever visit Greek islands? How about Melos? I see them disembarking, assisting excavations on the orchestra, drawing dental picks across flagstone crevices. Everything interests the Hardy boys; each event signals another step towards a resolution of the latest disappearance, burglary, kidnapping, smuggling, extortion, bribery…"'Looks like an ordinary rope to me,' Chet muttered. 'It does,' Frank agreed. 'But here's what I find particularly interesting. Notice that it's neatly spliced.'" The repetition of surprise, intrigue, revelation: this, too, becomes boring. Boredom's edges describe a universal unevenness; the proper text on boredom would be similarly uneven.

If one day from the same chalice we drink, let's make it absinthe.

Ramsey

Dear Franklin W. Dixon,

Riboflavin helps revitalize certain essential bodily processes, or so I'm told by a popular women's magazine. Advice columns, personal ads, commercials for under eye creams: the details that call attention to themselves never fully satisfy the desire to be attentive. In my desire to return to your books, I had wanted to write about purgation. The task should have been simple; already somewhat familiar with my topic, I wished to begin writing in the midst of purgation, to describe its contours from the inside out, to purge by inhabiting purgation. I began reading Siegfried Kracauer's essays: "People who still have time for boredom and yet are not bored are certainly just as boring as those who never get around to being bored." My project changed. Could I become purgation, or could I transcend purgation by purifying boredom? Perhaps I'm not explaining myself very well; somewhere I've read that Puritans slept together, everybody in one room. I'm reminded of the ornithopter, a flying machine engineered to fly under the power of its own flapping wings. Recall Leonardo's advice: "Dissect the bat, and concentrate on this, and on this model arrange the machine." I want to arrange a machine for boredom, I want gears and chambers, pistons and crankshafts to churn boredom out into parceled packages wrapped for the holidays. I want mechanized boredom to recreate its own methodologies: a method for crumpling, a method for forgetting, a method for disavowing long-held hopes. I want methods of boredom that even the Hardys couldn't crack, I want boredom coded and encrypted, I want boredom less pictorial than hieroglyphs, less alphabetical than phonetics. I want mechanized boredom to produce a method for cheating, for stubbing toes, a metaphorical method in which everything travels through grapes, a method for folding socks, for finding

Marilyn, a foreign method, a method for throwing stones. Boredom's tomb, cryptic boredom, mystical boredom, mythical boredom, boredom's mystical myths, mythical boredom riffs. I want my own flying machine, but unlike Leonardo, I don't want to get off the ground. Frank and Joe always end up underground, in cellars and subterranean passages. In one of your books, Chet takes up spelunking; in another, archaeology. Believing that he's made a significant find, he visits the Hardys, who explain that he has merely unearthed Aunt Gertrude's favorite sugar bowl, long missing after a picnic in the country. If only I understood the slippery potential for innuendo when I first read your books; uncovering Aunt Gertrude's favorite sugar bowl doesn't sound as innocent or foolish these days. If boredom has gone under-ground, I want to go with it. I want to talk about failure; I want letters to a nonexistent author of mostly offensive, occasionally entertaining literature aimed at "boys 10 to 14 who like lively adventure stories" to become failure, to fail to become what, in writing, every other attempt at boredom would also become: a portrait of boredom taken in failure. Remember the sadness of the birthday gift you couldn't properly assemble? These letters too must remain broken and dysfunctional, directions for the toy that never gets built.

I think of bandits; to you I suggest savoring aspic between nibbles of mutton.

Regards,

Ramsey

Dear Franklin W. Dixon,

Today my ovate thoughts won't radiate into the neat circle I'd much prefer. Let's capsulize some scattered attempts at circumscribing boredom's dubitable boundaries: the cardoon, a tall, thistle-like southern European plant related to the globe artichoke; the dolmen, a megalithic tomb with a large, flat stone laid horizontally across upright stones of comparable size; the hectograph, a device for copying documents by way of a gelatin plate. Nouns provide spaces for decay. The same boredom that prevails in times of great strain prevails in moments of relative idleness. The same law that compels salt to dissolve in water compels boredom to dissolve in passion. One pittance of boredom equals many bushels of labor. Theaters of boredom: an empty library, an abandoned school cafeteria, a park under reconstruction. Boredom's most frequent patrons ride elevators to the upper floors.

I'm tracing your initials in my notebook. Remember fill-in-the-blanks?

Ramsey

Dear Franklin W. Dixon,

According to ancient traditions, the four elements surrounded boredom; shrouded by bodies neither heavy nor light, boredom became an incorruptible vaporous mass into which materials collapsed. Torn apart by the bipolar pairs of the fourfold, even solids transformed, becoming dispersions of liquids: cataract spray, cloud spring, river mist. In *The Twisted Claw*, Frank and Joe report back to their father, Fenton Hardy, that a pirate named Cartoll has built an "island kingdom called the Empire of the Twisted Claw." Mr. Hardy is shocked: "An island kingdom called the Empire of the Twisted Claw, you say? What an amazing story!" The Hardys live out Pascal's observation that "Curiosity is only vanity," that "we usually only want to know something, so we can talk about it; in other words, we would never travel by sea if it meant never talking about it." When the Hardys stow away on one of the pirate's ships—the *Black Parrot*—they wind up bound and hooded, trapped in the cargo hold. I recapitulate these events, Mr. Dixon, not so much as reminders of what provokes interest or excitement in your readers, but to demonstrate what kinds of events fail to prevent a slippage into boredom in the midst of your books, despite the fact that I had originally sought, inside your texts, a refuge and a promise of excitement that might save me from considering desires otherwise unfulfilled. I'm bored with all this talk of slippage, gaps and absences, language's inadequacies, the fragmentary aspects of the smoothest story. Let's begin again with the Hardys, Frank and Joe. Let's revisit Bayport, Barmet Bay, the old boathouse, and the football field. Your plots steered clear of religion, politics, women; in the late fifties and early sixties, when your books began to resurface, your generic, agreeable storylines, your black and white versions of crime, must have seemed appealing.

At least the fourfold left room for fornication; in Bayport, even the ducks are square.

Ramsey

Dear Franklin W. Dixon,

The Hardy boys are always in motion, on the track, following up on leads, and everything goes through Bayport. Let me tell you that your small-town logic doesn't impede the overriding sense that behind every stranger, another criminal waits. Perhaps paranoia, the kind of permanent fear and suspicion your books encourage, provides the easiest method for short-circuiting boredom. Today I thought about calling my old drug dealer, getting high, scrupulously following the advice I find in Kafka's *Blue Octavo Notebooks*: "There is no need for you to leave the house," he writes. "Stay at your table and listen. Don't even listen, just wait, be completely quiet and alone. The world will offer itself to you and be unmasked...in raptures it will writhe before you." As I read these words, it seemed as if the plasma had been withdrawn from my blood, I became immobilized by the thought of speed and the need to regulate its powers with marijuana...but these desires are old enough and acute enough not to register as true boredom. Only Frank and Joe can get me there, and precisely because, at one time, they saved me from boredom that really did seem paralyzing. Your faith in the inevitable benefaction of repetitive practices impresses me.

Respectfully yours,

Ramsey

Dear Franklin W. Dixon,

Today I watched Oprah. In the company of boredom, morning makes the distance between buildings a density and a presence. The streets are pillows into which thoughts recline. Lamps inside the darkest houses diffuse pieces of light onto kingdoms of heavy air that boredom exudes. To find yourself in boredom, press your hands against your body, rub blood back into your muscles, wrap yourself in comfortable clothes. Boredom "becomes the only proper occupation," writes Kracauer, "since it provides a kind of guarantee that one is, so to speak, still in control of one's own existence." What kind of control does boredom impose? Your books, too, impose a kind of control: friends are "chums," counterfeit bills are "phony," angry characters are "miffed." Your words measure the separation between innocence and true crime; boredom separates individual and environment, it lowers a blind that allows for control. One's thoughts suggest that sensorial impressions will not suffice, that the surroundings won't bear the weight signifying requires. The empty sign is the only sign, and it appears everywhere, without mercy. And yet, these statements can't burglarize boredom's vault. Boredom can't be marked. Its contours alter themselves constantly. In language it's fugitive, metaphors only blur its corners, its structures rust and crumble under linguistic scrutiny, any effort to engage it in dialogue will only transform its substance, alter its contents, fabricate its identities; even boredom's originals are phonies. That's why I'm writing to you, Mr. Dixon. I'm amazed that boredom escapes me, just as it escaped Frank and Joe. I know what it feels like, I know it when I see it, I can record the places and processes that helped it to gain a foothold in my mind, but as soon as I try to put it into language, it's gone. I had wanted to write to you as one might write to an abstract noun, as a way of conjuring and conceptualizing spaces and territories, as a way of traversing the ground between us, as a way of familiarizing you; instead, your chambers seem ever more remote. I can't find you in my letters. I feel drawn to you all the more. I dictionary away your difficulties, the way your absence commands activity; under duress, under surveillance, under suspicion; I need to consider your willingness to hide. Factional legacies, fictional profligacy, proficiency, effectively expedient, appropriately ecstatic, ingeniously abstract, compulsively obtuse literary impulsivity: the air has a boredom, the room has a boredom. The rook: bored. The rune: bored. Ruing the boredom boredom brings. Reclining in the director's chair boredom brings. Boredom's progress, boredom's regress, boredom's egress. Boredom's labyrinth: a bull's eye. Boredom comes to rest inside a circle of diminishing circumference.

Consider these letters efforts to withdraw boredom from the pantheon of solvable mysteries.

Ramsey

Dear Franklin W. Dixon,

Do you remember Henry the Navigator, the Portuguese prince who planned excursions along the African coast? His efforts helped the imperial expansion of the Portuguese empire into Africa and the Far East. "Man's current quest," says Georges Bataille in *Visions of Excess*, "does not differ from those of Galahad or Calvin either in its object or in the disappointment that comes once the object is found." In boredom, the knowledge that effortful questing leads to disappointment cancels the impulse to embark. "I did as when I could not sleep," Beckett writes in his *Trilogy*, "I wandered in my mind, slowly, noting every detail of the labyrinth, its paths as familiar as those of my garden.... Unfathomable mind, now beacon, now sea." Frank and Joe always reach the end, grail in hand. They navigate effortlessly, mapping and tracking, tracing and overlapping the paths of crooks until they've been captured. "'Okay,' Frank said. 'The island we want is in the center of the group. After dark, Joe and I will use your rubber raft and paddle to the inlet we saw.'" I'm concerned with this navigational ease, this quick ability to appraise geographical forms. Every mountain and ridge tinted and shadowed, shown in relief, covered in radiating lines, every topographical inconsistency outlined, every elevation change registered and reproduced through mathematically accurate proportional representations, every shallow valley and undulating stream charted and sketched, grids, coordinates, keys and legends, indexes and surveys. No map can tell me how I made it to the store this morning, no track-tracing can reproduce the steps I took to get this letter into the mail. Maybe the Hardys and their rubber raft won't float down every inlet after all; if I stop reading your story before the case gets solved, if I get bored and put down your book, it's because I've stopped believing in your cartographies. Perhaps modernity generates, as Kracauer suggests, boredom as a phenomenon. Perhaps what I'm writing about can't be separated from ennui, but I was never able to translate that word with any confidence, and it doesn't stick to me the way boredom does. It belongs in someone else's city, not mine. A linchpin hitches boredom to technology's wheel. Boredom-as-axle greases my thought, recycling childhood under industry's smoke signals. I mention Henry the Navigator: the directionless desire under which boredom operates must be linked to the channel of energies directing his so-called explorations. When boredom reaches its threshold, potential actions arc toward violence. The slingshot, the catapult, the bow and arrow: Bataille explains that "energy is always in excess; the question is always posed in terms of extravagance. The choice is limited to how the wealth is to be squandered." Man, Bataille argues, must deal with excess, and this task "destines him, in a privileged way, to that glorious operation, to useless consumption." War is one outcome, among others; for me, boredom dispatches reason, reorders logic, and authorizes the letters I send you.

Please write back; even photogravures I make in your image need language to become animate.

Ramsey

Dear Franklin W. Dixon,

"Idleness," writes Kafka, "is the beginning of all vice, the crown of all virtues." I'm drawn to this formulation because it allows idleness to circulate at the beginning and ending of two opposing forms of behavior, so that idleness closes a circuit in which vice and virtue repeat, continuations of the same unproductive origin and endpoint. This futility cannot be matched; like Frank and Joe's Bayport, Kafka's idleness locks vice and virtue in a revolving system through which the reader might slip. Wrapped in Bayport, consumed by idleness, I find myself returning to the familiar travelogue boredom projects on the present. My room becomes an autobus, there are no other passengers, I'm stuck in traffic. The story of my fantasy unfolds in every letter, as a letter addressed to another part of myself. Or, maybe every letter is marked "Return to Sender." Idleness produces its own inscriptions, and if these letters can't enact idleness, at least they can trace its erasure. "In the most extreme case," Sandor Ferenczi's clinical diary reads, "activity withdraws even from the act of thinking." Lost in thoughts of the Hardy boys, thinking withdraws from the act of boredom. I'm prognosticating a solution, but the proof is missing.

Yours in fingerprints seen through a magnifying glass,

Ramsey

Dear Franklin W. Dixon,

The Hardys chase thieves to remote Caribbean Islands, radio back to Bayport, reclaim artifacts taken from the collections of small town museums. Ferenczi claims that after boredom descends, "What remains in the field of action is an unthinking playing with bodily organs, or allowing them to play (scratching, twiddling of moustache or thumbs, 'malmozni,' waggling of feet), and last but not least some kind of masturbatory genital activity." Still, Mr. Dixon, I'm sorry to say that I can't get it up for the Hardys. Perhaps they just don't bore me sufficiently. Every page invigorates certain boyhood memories, but they don't satisfy; the questions they raise incriminate me in ways I'd rather not say. Instead, let's talk about Frank and Joe, how I'm constantly reminded that siblings retain a primary power in your texts. This power can't be measured by Freud's triangular theories. Frank and Joe, like my brother and I, spend more time with each other than either one of them ever spent with their parents. Perhaps I'm losing my boredom because I'm losing my hold on where your books begin and I end, but isn't that what literature does to us all? According to Kracauer, in certain people the inability to access boredom arises when one's self disappears: "For their self has vanished," he writes, "the self whose presence, particularly in this so bustling world, would necessarily compel them to tarry for a while without a goal, neither here nor there." Thus Frank and Joe, constantly tricked into action by another mystery; thus my ongoing efforts to frame boredom in letters addressed to your nonexistence. In thick forests or vast fields in which sky overtakes the earth, glass blowers undoubtedly perceive every object according to its vitrescent potential. I don't want to turn boredom into glass, I want to drink from it, I want to be intoxicated again, but this time I don't have any money, and I don't want to pay for it. I'm a sophist, Mr. Dixon, but not because I don't know I'm wrong; I'd like to twist arguments like tourniquets, I'd like to stop the bleeding, but my logic's hopelessly hemophilic, and I'm running out of rags to dress my sentences. When I rode the school bus, I imagined the scenery outside without houses or buildings of any kind, I tried to see what the Natives might have seen; somehow, I couldn't understand that, with every home I disappeared, some portion of my boredom also vanished. Strange, then, when your placid Bayport domiciles also began to erode my boredom. I suppose they overtook the wilderness in my mind, and you must know that every invasion furnishes new materials conducive to something akin to consciousness, however distracted or colonized.

Wishing your books contained narcotics neither sedating nor stimulating,

Ramsey

Dear Franklin W. Dixon,

Today I searched the internet for solander boxes I intend to use for the safekeeping of your books. Designed by a Swedish botanist, solander boxes once held biological specimens; today, curators of aging collections use them to hold books. Remember when every class in school made time capsules? When Reagan was president, the need to preserve history for the handful of survivalists and their offspring who might make it through the apocalypse seemed significant. Every weather forecast conjured visions of clouds replaced by the trajectories of missiles across continents. Jet trails, amphibious vehicles, snow skis and dune buggies; evidence of the merger between machines for recreational and tactical purposes still startles me. On the news, Iraqis ride four wheelers across the desert, faces covered against blowing sand, Kalashnikovs in hand; cut to a Hummer commercial. Frank and Joe, teenage sleuths, use shortwave radios to bust the latest case. Is it any wonder that Kracauer recommends staying in as the latest advance in recreation? "On a sunny afternoon when everyone is outside," he advises us, "stay at home, draw the curtains, and surrender oneself to one's boredom on the sofa." Recall Bataille's belief in overabundance. Leisure time and war-time function, under his logic, as equal partners in the effort to waste excess energies and resources. The criminals attempt to get their share, but it's Frank and Joe who possess the privilege of excess.

Take up a new hobby: stay silent, stay still, let nothingness wash over you.

Ramsey

Dear Franklin W. Dixon,

Imagine a horse of miniature breed, kept by a falconer whose belief in healing achieved through absolute faith compels him to waste away under a medically treatable disease. Gums exuded by certain species of tropical plants, ocean currents that reappear in map legends as dashed lines denoting trade routes, barren land-scapes that belie great mineral rewards; these phenomena, nouns strung across verb-chains, invisible armatures that automate your story lines, enact criminal predictabilities: a transplanted turpitude, an overgrown trellis. We contrive every variety of fiction in order to obfuscate the nests where boredom dwells most naturally. Boredom accomplishes nidification (nest-building) by stealing materials left over after a diverse variety of activities, from paid labor to intercourse. Some nests remain visible. Others surprise us, arising just where we would anticipate excitement and interest. An emotional map of boredom reveals a nexus of adjacent perceptions and impressions: desire, exhaustion, play, intoxication, masturbation, comfort, interruption, nostalgia... "If, however, one has the patience, the sort of patience specific to legitimate boredom," Kracauer writes, "then one experiences a kind of bliss that is almost unearthly." Ferenczi suggests that something more than patience may be necessary: "What does being bored mean?" he asks. "Having to do something one hates and not being able to do what one would like: in any event a state of endurance." Patience, endurance, hatred, bliss; boredom, like concrete, solidifies in the shape of the forms that hold it in place. Parachuting into my thoughts this morning, three kinds of sea creatures: the sea anemone, the squirrelfish, the spiny dogfish. Like sprockets, thoughts turn in synchrony with chain-linked phrases, associations spring unbidden, mechanisms for analogical comparisons click into place. Boredom's awkward-fitting boot, boredom's pussy willow fluff, boredom's pumpkin skin, boredom's thick rind. The northern pufferfish, like my prose, inflates when threatened. I have no theory of boredom, only boredom, and I'm not foolish enough to stake any claims to authenticity.

Pulleys couldn't lift my discourse; I'm sinking into holes you helped me dig.

Ramsey

Dear Franklin W. Dixon,

Lost in a Mexican desert, Frank and Joe dig up a cactus and sip moisture that's collected somewhere near its roots. Remember when you thought you might get lost in a desert, and therefore ought to remember every step one should take in such a situation? The criminal *jefe* steals cattle and keeps explosives in his underground bunker. All Mexicans cheat and steal; it's Americans who can't tell a lie. The boys float iceboats on Barmet Bay, get bullied by Ike and Tad, find somebody's stamp collection. Desert dwellers known as resurrection plants survive droughts by folding up when dry and unfolding when moistened; I'd like to resurvey these letters for my own resurrection points, the places where my dry prose folds up, becomes boring. Monitoring my own respiration, I discover minute rattles at the deepest part of my lungs. I'm not concerned; I've inhaled enough lethal substances to assume that the aftereffects linger. Instead, it's the stethoscope that bothers me, and the dim recollection that I may have stolen it from a doctor's office—don't worry, Mr. Dixon, it was only a phase, as they say. I'm sure Frank and Joe wouldn't have done it, but I don't want to be Frank or Joe, I don't want to get in one of their damn planes, and I'm tired of mysteries getting solved. Does monitoring my own respiration bring on boredom, or cure it? My continual surprise in remembering that many of your books were written in the thirties: what depression? The Hardys take airplanes like the rest of us ride the bus. The alternative economic universes you privilege disparage the logic on which your mysteries are built.

Sincerely,

Ramsey

Dear Franklin W. Dixon,

I'd like to plant my own narrative inside this letter, transforming the circling, non-linear progression that typifies earlier efforts into a story driven by reportorial ambition. Think of all the songs you learned to play on recorder. Childhood knowledge, like boredom, recedes into the recto and verso progression of adulthood. Folding geometric prisms out of construction paper, watering the prickly pear your teacher brought back from break, peeking behind the art instructor who demonstrates at the potter's wheel, you glean information that turns you, at the proper age, into the perfect marionette. Let's stay away from clichés about puppets and strings; pick up some maracas, set a steady rhythm, reminisce about Mao. Where have all the communists gone? Remember the praying mantis, the mandolin, the cotton jumper? June bugs, too, have their place in whatever gallery we're fashioning. Ferenczi notes that, "Cases become difficult and pathological when the person who is bored is no longer aware of what he does or does not want." I'm not ready to pathologize my boredom; I'm tired of denying myself excess. It's boredom I want. What would Ferenczi say about that? I know what Kracauer would say: "Shrouded in tristezza, one flirts with ideas that even become quite respectable in the process...various projects that, for no reason, pretend to be serious." According to him, boredom underwrites my entire project. What am I doing, other than pretending to be serious? "Eventually," Kracauer continues, "one becomes content to do nothing more than be with oneself, without knowing what one actually should be doing." I'm writing to you because I want to be with myself. I don't know what I'm doing. And I'm the one who, as Kracauer puts it, "Harbors only an inner restlessness without a goal, a longing that is pushed aside, and a weariness with that which exists without really being." Isn't that you, Mr. Dixon? Aren't you precisely "that which exists without really being?" In *The House on the Cliff*, the Hardy boys investigate an old ghost that's said to haunt an abandoned mansion; in the end, it's only a young man who has lost his inheritance, who wants to occupy the house without the documents that would allow him to do so legally. You're in my house, Mr. Dixon. Your habits irritate me. Laura Hardy (Frank and Joe's mother) does next to nothing; in *The Mystery of the Flying Express*, she's mistakenly called Mildred. Frank and Joe never get anywhere with Callie Shaw and Iola Morton, respectively. Does it hurt to be so levelheaded?

Writing is one liability we share.

Ramsey

Dear Franklin W. Dixon,

Where would your books be without caves, underground rivers, trap doors, kidnappings, criminal syndicates, Chinese junks, candelabras, code names, jalopies, decoys? My parents built a bookshelf with hidden hinges that swung open to reveal a secret storage area. My cousin says it once held harvested marijuana plants. Was my dad a pot dealer who went straight? FDA planes buzzed over our property. When Reagan was president, the possible crimes your parents might commit were legion; the Cold War, the War on Drugs, the manufactured paranoia to which I'm dearly indebted for an imaginative childhood. Frank and Joe's friend Chet was fat and dim-witted; were there any stereotypes you outgrew? I imagine you smoked a pipe. Had you written a writer into one of your mysteries, he would've smoked a pipe. It's a given the writer would be male. What brand of moustache would he wear?

Questions perplex; answers dissatisfy. Here's to your anonymity,

Ramsey

Dear Franklin W. Dixon,

You wrote about fake stuff and didn't bother to make it seem real, so it was easier to imagine. Don't you think it's harder to imagine real stuff? Well, I don't mean to say you didn't imagine stuff really well. Take that sports car, for example, that Frank and Joe spin around in. What's not real about that? I don't blame you for teaching me to read and write. I just wish you could've lived outside yourself for a change—not like the newer Hardy Boys, when they started appearing in paperbacks with UFOs on the cover, but like Marlon Brando in *Apocalypse Now*, when he's babbling darkness to Dennis Hopper. Half-baked, overweight, incoherent—couldn't Frank and Joe get like that? High achievers burn out fast sometimes.

Somewhere kalmia blooms,

Ramsey

BURIAL RIGHTS:
SAN FRANCISCO, COLMA, AND THE DECOMPOSITION OF RECOLLECTION

1. Here lies...

A story of the cemeteries of 19th century San Francisco might begin with their demise: their dilapidated conditions increasingly drew the complaints of neighbors, and the occasional, unsanctioned disinterring of corpses did not please families of the deceased. The city passed a series of legal procedures that laid the groundwork for an enormous—if not bizarre—urban renewal project that would have a direct effect on an unexceptional community of farms directly south of the city, in an area that was first called "Lawndale."

The massive relocation of the buried remains of former San Francisco residents was needed, according to city officials and newspaper editorialists of the time, to rid the city of the terrible cemetery "winds" which resulted in "invisible effluvia that rise in the air from the cities of the dead," containing "gaseous poisons of the most deadly character."[12] It is possible that these cemeteries provided the material for the following description, written by Mark Twain for *The Adventures of Tom Sawyer*, published in 1876:

It was a graveyard of the old-fashioned Western kind. It was on a hill, about a mile and a half from the village. It had a crazy board fence around it, which leaned inward in places, and outward the rest of the time, but stood upright nowhere. Grass and weeds grew rank over the whole cemetery. All the old graves were sunken in, there was not a tombstone on the place; round-topped, worm-eaten boards staggered over the graves, leaning for support and finding none. "Sacred to the memory of" So-and-So had been painted on them once, but it could no longer have been read.[13]

In addition to their dilapidated conditions and the "invisible effluvia" that they emitted, the cemeteries of San Francisco occupied large portions of valuable open space. The amount of earth the city had reserved to bury its dead soon proved a hindrance to the land-hungry speculators seeking quick profits. Cemetery overcrowding resulted in the need for new burial grounds, at the same time that land throughout the city was becoming scarce.

"At night," wrote Walter Benjamin of a Paris train station, "one sees on the narrow unobtrusive benches... men stretched out asleep as if in the waiting room of a way station in the course of this terrible journey."[14] Perhaps it was Benjamin who also remarked, speaking of quotations, that they stand like epitaphs to mark the dead letter of the essay.

To recall the interring of the dead in early San Francisco—a haphazard process that resulted in the occasional reappearance of skulls during heavy rains, and that necessitated the eventual removal of tens of thousands of corpses—is to recapitulate the history of Western expansionism in miniature.

Perhaps the history of the American West is as one of Mark Twain's tombstones: it "stands upright nowhere."

In 1860, as part of an effort to avoid the spiraling costs of real estate in the city, the archbishop of San Francisco oversaw the opening of a new cemetery, six miles to the south. Over the course of the next seventy years, many remains would be buried or reburied in this suburban necropolis.

At the memorial for 35,000 unknown remains reburied at Cypress Lawn Memorial Park (most of them taken from what was formerly known as Laurel Hill Cemetery in San Francisco), a man whose exaggerated proportions are sculpted in bronze digs with a pointed spade while a woman rests nearby, a child in her lap. Behind them, wagon trains stretch out toward the two-dimensional granite horizon. Next to this family, a single obelisk reaches into the sky.

The man depicted in this monument calls to mind the unknown citizen-soldier of California's past, a mythic hero whose presence at the cemetery beckons to the future as well as to the recently deceased, asking that any and all take refuge at his side. The great capitalists who share the grounds beneath this bronzed laborer include Charles de Young (murderer of a man rumored to have slandered his mother, and founder of the newspaper that would become the San Francisco *Chronicle*), William Sharon (a millionaire who built his fortune on Nevada silver mines), Andrew Jackson Pope (an early timber baron), and William Randolph Hearst.

There is no mention of the Ohlone Indians, who once roamed the San Bruno Mountains that shield the park from the expressways to the west and east.

Even in these cemeteries, dug so as to accommodate the twice-laid-to-rest, eternity in this community has a remarkably short life. The nearby Cypress Hills Golf Course was built on top of what was Sunset View Cemetery; few graves, if any, were exhumed.[15]

2. Blessed are ye dead...

As the cemeteries of San Francisco moved southward, transporting bodies became a large source of revenue for the Southern Pacific Railroad Company. By 1887, funeral trains, complete with cars for coffins and mourners, made daily trips to the area. "Mourners, for 50 cents a person, made the trip in lush, somber, and comfortably appointed passenger cars. Caskets were transported in the baggage car for $1. By 1891, several transportation plans were offered on two daily scheduled trains."[16] In 1901, the Board of Supervisors of the city of San Francisco voted to disallow burials within city limits; by 1914, it had succeeded in evicting most cemeteries from the city entirely.

Michael Davidson: "Place is not a geographical or demographic entity so much as a conceptual field in which propositions of place are generated."[17]

In the massive effort to free the lands occupied by deteriorating bodies, hundreds of thousands of graves were dug up and moved to the "Lawndale" area. If families of the deceased could not pay for the cost of reburial, or could not be located, graves were simply covered over in the construction of new homes, parks, businesses, schools. City Cemetery would eventually become the California Palace of the Legion of Honor; Laurel Hill, once one of the city's largest cemeteries and home to some 38,000 remains, became the Richmond District, a sprawling, middle-class residential area.[18] "That 3,000 fewer bodies were exhumed than expected [from the Laurel Hill site] was never explained."[19]

Robert Duncan:

and here

let image perish in image,

leave writer and reader

up in the air

to draw

momentous

inconclusions...[20]

Unclaimed monuments and headstones from city cemeteries "were unceremoniously dumped in San Francisco bay... Others, along with elaborate stone work, were strewn along San Francisco's Ocean Beach..."[21]

Recall Susan Howe's dictum: "Historical imagination gathers in the missing..."[22]

In Sams Valley, Oregon, the unincorporated territory in which I spent my own childhood (and a territory ostensibly named after the English moniker adopted by—or assigned to?—a local Native leader, "Chief Sam"), a monument reminds those whose cars break down on Table Rock Road (for there is almost no other conceivable reason to stop at the commemorative stone) of the heroism of the U.S. Calvary, whose troops surrounded resistant members of Takelma Indians camped out above them on the cliffs of Table Rock. According to local legend, the standoff ended when members of the tribe leaped to their deaths.

Written across America, the history of this country thus appears as the unexpected plaque, interrupting the geometric pattern of the floor tiles in the local shopping mall, adorning an exterior wall of the county bank, or resting in shadows cast by the overpass of the freeway that leads out of town.

At Colma's Cypress Lawn Memorial Park, a large sundial marks the entrance. Egyptian themes are popular, in addition to the usual neo-classical flourishes and the ubiquitous California mission-revivalist gestures that adorn the most prominent park buildings, including mausoleums and the cemetery's Columbarium. The end result of such embellishments is to deflect the significance behind the monuments themselves, as if death were one more piece to be purchased by the keen curator with a penchant for attracting the largest possible audience.

Walter Benjamin's observation about fashion—that "What sets the tone is without doubt the newest, but only where it emerges in the medium of the oldest, the longest past, the most ingrained"[23]—undoubtedly holds true for cemeteries as well. The new cemeteries built to replace the decaying burial grounds of San Francisco strain insistently toward a nonexistent antiquity.

Might the production and exchange of history-as-commodity be understood as the ultimate grave truth that shapes the American West? At the Mission San Juan Bautista's visitor center in Central California, tourists might uncover a small sign stating that, "buried in this ground," "in unmarked graves," "are about 4,300 Mission Indians." A website dedicated to the Mission further underscores the degree to which the exploitative system of virtual slavery under which most missions functioned is ignored, explaining that these Indians "were friendly and came to help build the mission…. The Indians built all of the buildings and did nearly all the work…. The Indians at this mission liked the lifestyle so much that they needed to enlarge the church to hold 1,000 people."[24] These "Mission Indians" were from the Ohlone tribe, native to the San Bruno Mountains and the rolling hills of Lawndale, the burial grounds of San Francisco.

3. *To our dearly departed loved one...*

Importing remains from San Francisco, the Lawndale area grew by a curious sort of semi-permanent agriculture, the dead seeding its fertile soil. In 1941, residents of Lawndale were notified by the Post Office that a "Lawndale" already existed in Southern California; later that year, the town was rechristened as "Colma."

Robert Duncan:

> (*The President*
>   *orders history*
>   *reupholsterd*)
>   *Upon the sarcophagus of we know not whom,*
>   *each figure, impending, become a sign,*
>   *Perseus with the head in a wallet*
>   *turns his back and marches off...*[25]

In Atlanta's massive shopping complex named "Underground Atlanta," the locations of antebellum buildings are signaled by small plaques which, fortunately for retailers, are so unobtrusive that they hardly attract a second glance from shoppers, awed by the cavernous mall that stretches beneath the rapidly expanded city.

The intersection of history and commerce has become so complete that it is increasingly impossible to distinguish between the two: Is New York's South Street Seaport an historical site, or a mall? Can history as narrative exist without commerce?

"Interestingly, despite Colma's many millions of permanent residents, there is not a single ghostly tale or legend associated with the town."[26]

Consider the possibility that ghost stories are everywhere becoming more scarce, but leave open the possibility that there will be new ghost stories, stirred by the acceleration of technologies toward unpredictable ends. Read Wanda Coleman's poem, "Los Angeles Born & Buried":

> hear the automobile coffins? they drive crazy drive wild
> > glide noisily thru this
> burning smoggy sky and arid steel gray desert neath which
> > has been interred
> the beauty of my red beardless eagle-eyed forebears...
>
> yes, they abandon her to die, the men who have no power
> > leave her to the arms of
> still gray desert where she glides under sun in her sepulcher
> > on wheels
> > > drives crazy drives wild...

Perhaps the ghosts are already here—perhaps they are the ones behind the wheel. Ezra Pound: "where the dead walked / and the living were made of cardboard."[27]

Imagine purchasing a permanent residence in Colma. Do not be deterred by the fact that certain plots have proved less than permanent. Such developments create the possibility that your remains will become unknown, will join the "imaginary community" Benedict Anderson locates in the tomb of the unknown soldier:

No more arresting emblems of the modern culture of nationalism exist than cenotaphs and tombs of Unknown Soldiers. The public ceremonial reverence accorded these monuments precisely because they are either deliberately empty or no one knows who lies inside them, has no true precedents in earlier times.... Yet void as these tombs are of identifiable mortal remains or immortal souls, they are nonetheless saturated with ghostly national imaginings.[28]

What could be more American than the processions of Cypress Hill, Sunset View, Hoy Sun? As William Carlos Williams reminds us,

> *It is only in isolate flecks that*
> *something*
> *is given off*
> *No one*
> *to witness*
> *and adjust, no one to drive the car*[29]

Colma, like the New Jersey from which Williams writes, is filled with luminary halos of the city that always exists just beyond the horizon.

Despite the precision cut by the lines on the page, there is a sense that the locus of control is somehow outside the imaginary space from which the poem materializes: "The cleavage goes through all the phases of experience," Williams writes. "I mean only to emphasize the split that goes down through all the abstractions of art to the everyday exercises of the most primitive types—"[30]

At the fringes of the city, space refuses to compose itself into blocks that can be conveniently measured in square feet; seeping outward, the remainders of social and environmental inequalities seek out openings or subdivide into smaller and smaller pieces in order to claim space. Proliferation and accumulation of supplementary effects cause more proliferation and accumulation while still, anywhere and everywhere, one senses that something is lacking. Suburb and cemetery converge.

It is just as Gertrude Stein says it is: "It is very much like it."[31]

The sensation of becoming lost in the suburban neighborhoods that surround San Francisco unfolds in reverse: moving forward, one is immediately aware that what lies ahead is what lies behind, replicated to infinity. The breaking of new ground in such developments foretells the reburial of the already dead in the city of Colma, because the imagined community of unnamable masses who will inhabit the new houses is already known— indeed, it is already there: in Westchester, Long Island, Orange County, Palm Beach, the residents of the new suburb are already dwelling....

From the *Introduction to Computer-Assisted Experimentation*:

> Memory units do not accept and read out data instantaneously; a finite amount of time must elapse between the time the memory location is addressed and the time that the data can reliably be read from that location.[32]

Memory is still business in California; half an hour south of Colma, Silicon Valley companies steal secrets from one another in the ongoing competition to compress memory into the smallest possible computer chips. The "isolate flecks" that define our momentary perceptions do not fit neatly onto the monuments that mark the mass graves in Colma, but they can be written into tweets and twitters and the future memory of the internet. In the immediacies that govern perceptions and reactions, that infect memories and insert themselves into one's consciousness, particles divide and reconvene into progressively smaller and more obscure units, as if a fractal geometry of human experience could inevitably escape itself, elude definition, never be revealed for "what it is."

"I then spoke to Peters and to Parker," writes Edgar Allen Poe, "neither of whom returned my answer. Shortly after this period I fell into a state of partial insensibility.... I had the greatest difficulty in bringing to recollection the various circumstances connected with my situation..."[33]

What happens when the immediate familiarity of the present overwhelms the ability of the subject to frame his or her experience in language? What happens when "what is" appears to be exactly like what just was? When the "new development" appears to be an exact replica of the old development, relocated?

Take a simple reburial, for example, the same old bones. Whose bones are they if they can be moved around like chess pieces? Everywhere the West is plagued by the mythic frontiersman, overseeing the erection of cardboard tombs for suburbanites already living there or elsewhere...

Which on account if without flavor [writes Stein,]
Shall they be shamed with generation
They can leave it half as well.
I wish to remind everybody nobody hears me
That it makes no difference how they do
What they do...[34]

Can this be the new destiny? The new superfluidity of environments, the unobstructed flow of sameness? The "pure" production of the nameless and faceless dwellers transplanted to unfamiliar ground, only to be confronted by a strange familiarity that infects the "new" spaces these dwellers inhabit?

4. *O Death...*

As foreign as the latest resident of Bakersfield is to her new home, she recognizes the McDonalds and knows immediately the flavor and price of her microwaved life. In Colma, the uncomfortable proximity to the dead is balanced by the comfortable proximity to freeway ramps, gently winding car-commercial roads, stop lights, and chain stores. The Chamber of Commerce is located in a rectangular, concrete and glass commercial building. Ask directions to this nondescript locale, and the Sizzler restaurant across the street is given as the point of reference.

"In Colma, funeral processions have the right of way. Cutting into line was made illegal in 1929."[35]

This law does little to prevent the interruption made visible by the funeral procession itself, which leads to the ultimate resting place that, though it has been exiled from the city of San Francisco, waits at the end of every block for its next initiates: "In Colma, death is a part of daily life. Black hearses, often accompanied by motorcycle escorts, lead...seemingly endless funeral processions."[36]

Although reserving the right of way for funeral processions might sound like a potential logistical nightmare, in fact, the town of Colma is so small that traffic cannot be much of a problem. Split into its "unincorporated" and "incorporated" parts, its shopping centers and cemeteries, respectively, there is little threat that a procession will interrupt the flow of commerce.

The boundary between these two spaces is not marked; as Walter Benjamin writes of Paris, "As threshold, the boundary stretches across streets; a new precinct begins like a step into the void—as though one had unexpectedly cleared a low step on a flight of stairs."[37]

Drive north or south on El Camino Real, the corridor of stoplights that runs from San Francisco through Colma to San Jose, and you will discover a seamless stretch of suburban enclaves whose boundaries are invisible except for the signs notifying motorists of new municipalities. The watery extension of houses, filling cracks in hillsides and collecting at the lowest points, seems to fulfill the simplest laws of nature, at the same time that the ubiquitous, superfluous quality of the construction would seem to violate those selfsame laws.

Recall the houses described by Nathaniel West in *The Day of the Locust*:

> But not even the soft wash of dusk could help the houses...
> When he noticed that they were all of plaster, lath and paper,
> he was charitable and blamed their shape on the materials used.
> Steel, stone and brick curb a builder's fancy a little, forcing him
> to distribute his stresses and weights and to keep his corners
> plumb, but plaster and paper know no law, not even that of
> gravity.[38]

Defying gravity, such houses stretch toward another dimension beyond the dimension that holds those who dwell in their interiors. Perhaps it is this strange synthesis of aquatic and plastic characteristics—the tendency for the suburb to appear as if it had simply assumed the shape of the objects with which it is surrounded, at the same time that it appears to have been created out of nothing real, and to have created the things that surround it from this same unreal substance—that allows the suburb to be always exterior to itself, to have no center, to repel inquiry.

It may even be the case that this exteriority, this being foreign even as it is being itself, makes the suburban also somehow supraurban; it is neither here nor there, he nor she, we nor they.

Inside the Cypress Lawn Memorial Park Main Office, a waiting room of white couches and cherry wood armchairs surrounds a small coffee table, on which rests the self-published history, *Cypress Lawn: Guardian of California's Heritage.* "As both Cypress Lawn and its clients built memorials and commissioned fine art," the book states, "this collective process gradually transformed the Colma hillside to a place of grand beauty."[39]

This statement reveals something fundamental to the ethos that defines Colma: in a town built by the cemetery industry, the landscape serves as the raw material out of which to fashion a sprawling commercial complex of mausoleums, crematoriums, cenotaphs, crypts, sepulchers, mass graves.

With the uniformity promised by commercialism, at the same time that the suburban is neither here nor there, it is also here and there, the other and itself at the same time. The spread of strip malls and cardboard houses is happening not only in real time, but exponentially, because each addition is itself at the same time that it is more than itself, it is also all its other identical selves, a fact of which its inhabitants are increasingly, uncomfortably aware.

When your children have grown and you have relocated to an age-appropriate living environment, have them take you golfing at Cypress Hills Golf Course. Admire, from this hillside haven, the reiteration of graves across the opposite hillsides, and even closer to you, just beyond the rough, where signs alert you to the fact that balls hit into the cemetery are out of play. This is the end: plot your burial amidst talk of backswings, titanium putters, and the copyrighted dimple designs of competing golf ball brands. Admire, as you wait to take your last tee shot, the low hum that rises over the ridge behind you, the hum of highways and housing developments and hopeful children whisked through yellow lights by parents bearing the self-assured grins of new home security system owners. This is California, *this* is, this *is*—the end.

NOTES

12. Quoted by Michael Svanevik and Shirley Bugett's *City of Souls: San Francisco's Necropolis at Colma* (San Francisco: Custom and Limited Editions, 1995), 33.

13. *The Adventures of Tom Sawyer* (New York and London: Harper and Brothers, 1903) 100-101.

14. Walter Benjamin, *The Arcades Project*, trans. by Howard Eiland and Kevin McLaughlin (Cambridge and London: BelknapPress of Harvard University Press, 1999), 86.

15. *City of Souls: San Francisco's Necropolis at Colma*, 124.

16. ibid., 29.

17. Michael Davidson, *The San Francisco Renaissance: Poetics and Community at Mid-century* (New York: Cambridge University Press, 1989), 125.

18. Today, the only open space left over from the days of Laurel Hill Cemetery is a children's playground of the same name, miniscule in comparison to the original size of the cemetery.

19. *City of Souls: San Francisco's Necropolis at Colma*, 43-44.

20. Robert Duncan, "Where it Appears, Passages 4," *Bending the Bow*, 15.

21. *City of Souls: San Francisco's Necropolis at Colma*, 45.

22. Susan Howe, *Frame Structures: Early Poems, 1974-1979* (New York: New Directions, 1996), 3.

23. *The Arcades Project*, 64.

24. http://www.cuca.k12.ca.us/lessons/missions/Bautista/ SanJuanBautista.html#community

25. Robert Duncan, "Passages 30, Stage Directions," *Bending the Bow*, 131-132.

26. *City of Souls: San Francisco's Necropolis at Colma*, 12.

27. Ezra Pound, *The Cantos* (New York: New Directions, 1993), 814.

28. Benedict Anderson, *Imagined Communities* (London: Verso, 1983), 9.

29. William Carlos Williams, *Imaginations* (New York: New Directions, 1970), 133.

30. ibid., 133-135.

31. Gertrude Stein, *Stanzas in Medition* (Los Angeles: Sun & Moon Press, 1994), 59.

32. Kenneth L. Ratzlaff, *Introduction to Computer-Assisted Experiment-ation* (New York: John Wiley & Sons, 1987), 44.

33. Edgar Allen Poe, *The Collected Tales and Poems* (New York: The Modern Library, Random House, 1992), 804.

34. *Stanzas in Meditation*, 158.

35. *City of Souls: San Francisco's Necropolis at Colma*, 3.

36. ibid., 11.

37. *The Arcades Project*, 88.

38. Nathaniel West, *Miss Lonelyhearts & The Day of the Locust* (New York: New Directions, 1950), 61.

39. *Cypress Lawn: Guardian of California's Heritage* (Hong Kong: Cypress Lawn Memorial Park, 1996), 25.

2

SERGEANT PEPPER'S METER MAID:
LETTERS FROM BERKELEY

Dear Sergeant Pepper,

For a long time now I've been convinced that drugs construct a link to history's underside. LSD conjures the Sixties; prewar Vienna reclines in cocaine's powdered foothills. On the cover of the album that bears your name, Edgar Allen Poe, Sonny Liston, Sigmund Freud. I write to you because this album forms, along with co-op peanut butter and carob chips, patterns my dreams make into quilts and fold over childhood's pillows. I'm writing to you because half-baked concepts define my labor; my pallid inspiration can't access completion. Experts consider your *Lonely Hearts Club Band* an unfinished concept album. Visionary excess never completes its projects, but its leavings provide ample room for the inebriations that others call entertainment. As a decade, do the Sixties match this pattern? All I know today dissolves in water, fits into my medicine cabinet, contours deformities in bone and muscle. The mannequins on your album cover remind me that all knowledge is orthopedic.

Thanks anyway for your well-boiled optimism,

Ramsey

Dear Sergeant Pepper,

In mornings rain converts to caverns I paint buffalo on igneous walls my mind makes. Waiting for the coffee to percolate, I watch neighbors shepherd children into cars. The lunchbox deserves more respect as an object. I don't know what my neighbors do, no one here seems to have a job, empty storefronts line thoroughfares. The town is a great obscurantist; its mystique arises from the walled-in nature of its being, the fact that borders order its existence. Berkeley, California, virtual incubator, petri dish for the experiments they call family life, begets its own breed of progenitors. Parenthood in Berkeley signals infantilism's rediscovered popularity. In Berkeley only bodies age, dressing themselves in wrinkles California sun perfects for its palest conquerors, karmic revenge for winters spent out-of-doors, sampling warmth: fogged-in warmth, post-rainfall asphalt-inspired warmth, warmth lifting as mist from backyard gardens, warmth as smiles Berkeley residents share like sugar-free mints. The entire town fashions itself humanity's compost, preserving its degradable waste for future generations. Sergeant Pepper, I write to you because it's 2007, and although I have now lived through three of them, I don't know what to do with decades. The Sixties, your decade, belong to me, but not like a lunchbox belongs to a hand; I'm thinking about burnt matches, coffee grains. I don't have the energy to use them as fertilizer, but I can't get rid of them either: that's the Sixties. They refuse to leave me alone, they lead me into half-hearted metaphors. As a decade I didn't inhabit, the Sixties mark the other side of my beginning—the years my parents became themselves, or someone did. I write to you because I live in Berkeley, fairy godmother of the Sixties. I write you letters because I've never been much for deltiology—postcards mark voyages. I seek the permanent imprint, the definitive stamp. On the other hand, fugacity interests me most, and your title epitomizes the impermanence my letters cannot match. They strain for significance, for duration. Sergeant Pepper, nomenclature withheld, origin unknown, corresponding body unspecified: your shifting identities expose my desire for stability.

Here's to chasing vulgarities in gas masks,

Ramsey

Dear Sergeant Pepper,

I remember driving my pregnant wife to San Francisco. The inevitability of parenthood dissipated in evening traffic; the Bay Bridge's tunnel through the island that marks its midsection must be an unusual feature for bridges, or so I mused, focusing my eyes on the minivan in front of us. I recollect this bit of half-spoken dialogue to remind you that instants might be composed of something—might contain details, like cacti. Instants are succulents I said to my wife, the jade tree or friendship tree, *Crassula ovata*, instants can't overtake the gardens our minds leave un-watered, but they can be rediscovered long after other vegetation acquiesces to the inevitable. Just drive she replied, just drive. Sergeant Pepper, I'd like to focus on my concern with the inevitable, with parenthood, but minivans and traffic keep me preoccupied. While my wife and my mother-in-law watched theater, I enjoyed an illicit massage; my ejaculation heralded guilt. Later, in a used bookstore, I came upon Jonathan Weiners' *Hotel Wentley Poems*, a first printing of the original chapbook sitting in a broken wooden bin. I did not buy it but wondered instead about my ongoing inability to purchase the transgender escort I'd likely prefer to the female prostitutes I normally imagine myself frequenting. When my wife and I met, we were living in Brooklyn. It was 2001. I was teaching third grade, and I had a student named Julius who took it upon himself one day to share with the class everything that he knew about gender and sexuality. Sometimes, Julius explained, a boy wants to be a girl, and sometimes a girl wants to be a boy. Julius' father was a surgeon, and it turned out that Julius knew a lot about this topic, especially when it came to surgery. "My dad says it's easier to dig a tunnel than to build a bridge," Julius told the class. The Bay Bridge is a transgender structure, both bridge and tunnel I tell myself, a reflection of the escort I can't purchase. Like certain writers I have met, whose works I have most admired—but to whom I can barely speak when introduced—it seems that any direct encounter with the object of desire stifles my language. Others identify my silence as shyness; your name induces similar results. A Sergeant, but a forgiving one, tuned to humanity's celebrated dissatisfaction. Waiting for my wife to emerge from the theater, I bought a cup of coffee and witnessed a panic attack: a woman, about my age. Emergency personnel lifted her into the ambulance while I ogled. I reminded myself, apropos of nothing, that the vases we own sit on high shelves, awaiting flowers we don't buy.

Wishing I could play self-hating Jew to a rewarding audience,

Ramsey

Dear Sergeant Pepper,

We share impulses toward mysticism, but your mysticism conceals militarism; mine disguises adolescent drug use. On your album cover I remember blue and jackets. The sky dominates faces of people I don't recognize, save The Beatles. My high school English teacher, Mr. Wixon, once told me Edgar Allen Poe could be found in the back row. Today I review your cover art to confirm his claim. Lapels, like castanets, remind me that not all nouns bear equal weight. You signal a decade I can't translate, ideological static. The only military man I recall: "Lovely Rita." When I first listened to your music, rubber bands, like paper clips, seemed vital to me; repositories of mystery, they possessed physical abilities neither anthropomorphic nor mechanical. A *Lonely Hearts Club* band couldn't match the importance of a rubber one. Sergeant Pepper, Buffalo Bill, Rocky Raccoon, entities necessarily child-friendly, pairing foodstuffs or animals with smart handles. Music informed me of movements my parents' stories confirmed, but I confused. Civil Rights, anti-war, feminism, Stonewall: buttering my pancakes, history melted into whole wheat. My parents, back-to-the-land, built their own home, grew vegetables. I suffered through haircuts my mother administered: the bowl, a coiffure-based mistake that condenses my entire childhood. Today my wife and I, exhausted, took our socks off in the living room and left them on the floor. Socks on carpet testify to the pleasure lethargy brings. Indecent, the socks gestured to memory's pinfeather: my father considered socks on the floor a personal insult. Today, I understand his extremism. He built the floor himself. Rejections of consumerism my parents made I can't match, but I claim my own forms of guilt. On the way home from work, I stop at an overpriced grocer for pre-made salads—signature dinners for yuppies—and organic apples. In the dairy isle, a student of mine from the after school program I work in, reminder of my half-assed employment, reads cheese labels to her mother. I can't remember anyone's name, but in Berkeley spices are eponyms: Sage, Rosemary, Juniper, Cinnamon. I don't know how to build houses or, like my mother, diagnose diseases. I feel life as something worth fumbling, or rather, I find myself fumbling. I want desperately to succeed in recalling the purpose behind my misplaced desires, but this hope, like the Mississippi, signals a flow and not an expulsion. I am writing a theory of frustration; I call it "letters." The cassette tape that played your music in the deck of our Civic hatchback became stretched and distorted. Remember facts of the eighties? Sun through a car's windshield warps cassette tapes. "When I'm Sixty-Four" drones into drunken garble. As a kid I wondered what army you called your own; the image on the tape's cover didn't help me. In a testament to technology's redundancy, my parents also had your LP. Contemplating the cassette tape's resignation—inevitable—signals desire's unquenchable thirst. We want things that last, but not for too long. Recently I have begun resigning myself, a process I call inevitable. My mediocre career, my history of entry-level jobs. My ability to forget lyrics. I don't like The Beatles, not enough to share in fandom's inanity. Fans share conversations the way parents trade witticisms about children. Holding on to commonalities that initiate dead-end dialogues, they strain for subtle gestures of superiority: the run-in with a band member, the eldest son's summer camp exploit. Sergeant Pepper, today I write because I hate children, but only because Berkeley parents irritate me, especially those who insist upon your music as childhood's balm. Reeking of marijuana, a parent arrives to pick up his third-grader. Does his inebriation signal antiwar rallies, jazz clubs, conspiracies Weathermen hatch? He fumbles with a

pen, signs something, wanders after his child and out the door.
Mao died in 1976, the year before my birth; I would become a
monk whose faith is built upon this fact, but I smoked my faith
in joints rolled to commemorate marijuana's historical import.

From Berkeley, Halicarnassus of the Sixties,

Ramsey

Dear Sergeant Pepper,

I think I fail in my effort to articulate the importance my inconsistent work history should bear in letters addressed to your
irresolute image. I want to carve out of my indigence a metaphor
your music makes evident. I'm insisting upon parenthood and
Berkeley, theme and location, to administer treatments lost
decades deserve. I invoke your image because you figure in
myths from which marketers still profit; heralding change, you
usher conservatism in through the back door. What does this
skullduggery have to do with my inconsistent employment? Let's
let this question linger over the racket Berkeley kids make on
their way home from school, parading upper-class privilege in
pageants starring immigrant nannies who tote knapsacks and
cello cases. A friend tells me that what they call "tracking" keeps
Berkeley High teenagers busy on weekends: promising material
rewards, boyfriends prostitute girlfriends to classmates. We live
in Lorin, southernmost outpost of Berkeley—a neighborhood
bordering Oakland, and edging ever closer to gentrification.

Walking the dog past neighbors whose skin color doesn't match my own, I wonder what my whiteness means. Is your music anything more than a piece of material evidence, part of the cultural archive that marks my racial privilege? My fugitive paychecks suggest shortcomings that histories of oppression can't explain.

Only witches drink Strega; temper your thirst with Ativan.

Ramsey

Dear Sergeant Pepper,

Today I think that parenthood—the anxiety it brings—has everything to do with lost limbs and photographs. Think about pictures you throw out, extras that don't belong in the scrapbook. Once, for a birthday party, my friends and I attended an exhibition basketball game. Afterwards, with my new camera, I had a chance to have my picture taken with Clyde "The Glide" Drexler. Then I photographed each one of my friends with him. Every time, I cut my friend out of the picture; you can see a friend's arm, disappearing behind Clyde's back, and you can see Clyde, smiling amicably. Clyde's arm slants toward the edge of the picture, embracing a body that's not there. Parenthood must be like this body, the one left out of the picture, the one you know someone reaches toward. I'd like to safeguard the pleasures of delinquency and transgression from the vacuous respectability that parenthood insinuates. I fantasize an underground chamber that connects homes to demimondes, that refigures the domestic as momentary respite from life's disreputable constants. Take my indolence, for example; I ought to descend into my hypogeum, where hoodlum friends consider torpor a virtue. Instead, I linger on Berkeley's overgrown side streets, looking through ferns at discarded apple cores. Tie-dyed, my imagination staggers against concrete: what I can't fathom concerns the Sixties as ideological collapse, liberalism's last hurrah. Agent Orange, Napalm: chemical warfare announces realities that Berkeley's gardeners, masked against allergens and preening roses for competitions, can't answer. This town refigures the great depression as what happens when radical thinkers earn enormous wealth. Strapped for revolutionary ideas, rich intellectuals cradle glasses of pinot noir and ponder investments in third homes. Today I visit the independent bookstore; in the poetry section, I stumble across half-assed efforts; young, self-admiring self-starters smartly address their unreadable poems to similarly self-satisfied peers. Nobody wants thinking anymore, they want companionship. Everyone acts as if clocks give shape to meaning. Try indolence, I want to say; let laziness take over. Grow weeds, not flowers. People seem to think that a little hard-won leisure time means they're not wrecking everything worthwhile by turning tricks at the capitalist fuckholes they call jobs. And what do you care, Sergeant Pepper? Today I prefer *The Supremes*, but I'll return my lonely heart to you after the half-dead ex-hippies that run this hellhole sell the last stock they need in order to buy another fucking ski lodge. Until then, I reserve my malaise for me alone.

Don't write back, call me; I want to hear your voice, "Turning again," as Jacques says in *As You Like It*, "toward pipes and whistles."

Ramsey

Dear Sergeant Pepper,

Please excuse the theatrics of my last letter; drinking wine, I refashion Berkeley's debilitation as my own. My father watched *Easy Rider* in Huntsville, Texas, soon after its release, in 1969. He tells me that, at the climax of the movie, the murder of Wyatt and Billy (Peter Fonda and Dennis Hopper, respectively) brought cheers from the crowd. The lesson isn't that Texans don't like hippies; it's that things are not, as John and Yoko understood, "getting better all the time." David Farragut—commander of the U.S. Navy during the Civil War—conjures no memory for me when, stepping toward the bakery, I see a flier that bears his name. The flier lies in the gutter, evidence that the lecture to be delivered on the long-deceased commander's exploits might not garner the audience that lecturers desire. Everyone in Berkeley has a favorite bakery, save me. Nonetheless, approaching the counter at our neighborhood bakery, I adopt an air of admiration, enthusiasm. What I don't like about baked goods is the temporarily heated—but now room-temperature—trajectory of their existence. The bakery is the culinary version of the Sixties. Crusted with an apparently impenetrable, seemingly admirable communal spirit, baking's promise ends in domesticity. I listen as patrons trade stories of garlic presses and filleting techniques. This, Sergeant Pepper, is where the Sixties have landed: the Whole Earth Catalogue as sold by Williams and Sonoma. I want my LSD in the water supply where it belongs, I want psychedelia to reclaim terrorism as its proper ground. I'll buy any pastry infused with hallucinogens; it's the sugar and cooked fruit I can do without.

Good luck garnering cheers when they learn that your band has only an intro and its reprise,

Ramsey

Dear Sergeant Pepper,

In an antique store nearby, a dealer explains that the device in my hand combs noils out of wool before spinning. Inevitably, he says, someone asks; I haven't asked, but his explanation drags on, regardless. I resign myself to the inevitable. I make myself a sign of the inevitable: it's the sun or some such, a mythic thing hieroglyphs capture. Back at home, I sketch an image. Later, in front of my students, I display my drawing. My students admire what I sketch because they don't know what sketching should be. The inevitable confronts me in children's linguistic contortions; they speak in time's language, the voice portending death's approach. "Scientifically," my mother likes to say. Whenever she says *scientifically*, an explanation follows. A great believer in science, she considers many events inevitable; words attach themselves to people, people to words; "inevitable" clings to my mother. I don't mind the inevitable; I've resigned myself to antique theories, and to death, the voice its usher. Nonetheless, many parents seem hesitant to introduce the inevitable to children, hedging death with artificial sweeteners, religion, superheroes. Sergeant Pepper, I don't mind death, but California's syrupy residue nauseates me. My former place of residence: New York City. I try to adjust to Berkeley by reminding myself that surroundings can't erase lifelong proclivities. My wife's pregnancy signals an acquiescence, one we both acknowledge, to Berkeley's domesticity. In Berkeley, everybody's pushing some stroller, pedaling a bike behind which a child-transporting device trails, navigating the three streets that lead somewhere in cars strapped down with safety seats, gliding along train station escalators, hand-in-hand with the next generation's commuters. Nonetheless, in a year or two, as soon as my wife finishes her graduate school coursework, we're going back to New York. All these families in transit can't disguise the return of the Fifties, conservatism clad in progressive fabrics. We may buy hemp socks, but our homes have security systems that military men designed.

When I throw my no-hitter, I want your kid to make the last out.

Ramsey

Dear Sergeant Pepper,

Wandering a Berkeley side street, I stop at a fence made from old Volvo hatchbacks. One thing I notice here: no one reads. Crafts and baking, gardening and antiquing, leave little room for books. In New York you see people reading all the time, on the subway, in the park. New Yorkers make of reading an activity, the way Berkeley residents ride bicycles, but even on the subway New Yorkers read gracefully. Berkeley's timelessness—the fact that its residents group-sing songs written to protest injustices that the rest of the world has long since forgotten—also defines its influence on adults, whose demeanors, hobbies, stances, and modes of being in the world remain impaired by the town's Dr. Seussian atmosphere. The skateboard maintains a popularity with people Jerry Rubin would have called old. And while I too favor transportation alternatives, the image certain folks cut—their unshapely silhouettes lumbering by, teetering over the thin frames of undersized bicycles—leaves me aesthetically underwhelmed. Bicycle helmets remain uncool, and even if they declare safety, the relative risk posed by Berkeley's half-dead chronically empty suburban avenues renders most headgear superfluous. A gnu and a wildebeest are one and the same. An ocarina is also known as a sweet potato. Nonetheless, common meanings rescue language from redundancy. Choosing between inebriation and crapulence, I try my hand at both—albeit via different, similarly illegal substances. Like children whose fears lurk under beds or behind closet doors, the adults that claim Berkeley as their place of residence localize fear in unexceptional places. The plastic water bottle, the neighbor who smokes cigarettes on the porch, the contents of the day care center's cabinets; each of these entities has its role as the monster that Berkeley parents fear most. What concerns me today: my resignation to the conventional. In Berkeley, the best I can do is to feign my resistance, let fall a few snide comments; meanwhile, the current carries us—inevitably, it seems—toward some other, more monstrous, conservatism. Consider the missionary position, parenthood's sexual equivalent; if we can't find our way out of this place, we'll all be fucked. I like kids, but I don't want to wake up to my own children singing "When I'm Sixty Four."

With mortal and pestle I grind out these letters,

Ramsey

Dear Sergeant Pepper,

This morning I rose like a Morisco, wrapped in religious oaths addressed to someone else's god. My wife craves mortadella; I know where to buy it in Brooklyn, but I can't find it in Berkeley. Is this our fate, to seek a mortadella that never comes, to drive in circles for a mortadella that may not exist? Or, like mortadella itself: amidst a soft, pink condensation of leftover meats, to take delight in the occasional pistachio. The moon still out as morning broke, I wandered with the dog toward stanchions that make of our street a virtual cul-de-sac. The health food my parents fed me made baloney verboten. I want to make an observation to illustrate the world that misses you—and that you're missing, blissed out somewhere, craving stardom, but reveling in its recession: I like to think of you as the John and Paul dyad that never existed, a perfectly amicable all-male union. Perhaps that's why I write you these letters: I recognize that, in addressing you, I have not one audience, but two. What's more, I envision you as the homosocial unit I can't access through my marriage. Nonetheless, these features make you neither wise, nor receptive; in fact, they make you remote, a transcendent figure, and one that only drugs allow me to contemplate with any precision. Think of the Sixties, humanity's public answer to centuries of secret indulgences. Berkeley bakers mimic the Sixties in vegan brownies and innovative pizzas: toppings include nettles, oysters, aged cheeses, raw eggs. Suburban planning constrains car traffic; stop signs bear graffiti against driving. These aren't observations, they're anti-spiritual rants that mistake precise language for blows against the idiocy others call religion. Or politics. In fact, what I desire most this morning: a cane. Not to help me walk, but to swing through the air or wave at passersby. Yes, some college students lurk around certain Berkeley streets, but once you leave the critical center the university thinks it marks, everything's transformed by kinship's mysterious caverns. Suburban and subterranean, the Berkeley family stakes its claim to generational roles by turning maturation on its head. Children, fonts of wisdom, enforcers of tradition, face attention-deficient parents who can barely focus on the outdoor hobbies that distract them from more pertinent tasks. It's parents who show no signs of maturity. I stand in the front yard of the home that houses our apartment; overhead, the Goodyear blimp floats; a football game draws cars to the stadium up the hill. Who doesn't want to be like that blimp? In your songs and movies that feature them, anything becomes a dirigible; airborne, contagious, I drift toward failed serums, imagination galvanized by former intoxications I don't want to rediscover, so much as understand, anew; reenacting failure, I remember the bum acid I purchased at arts and crafts fairs masquerading as hippie revivals. Let's make a pact to commemorate failure through two-word phrases. The Sixties, for example.

To hangovers, salves for egos overheated by alcoholic confidence.

Ramsey

Dear Sergeant Pepper,

The sweatshirt—Berkeley's favorite fashion piece—remains in vogue, even if its long-heralded successor, the fleece pullover, maintains a majority in the well-heeled districts toward the hills, and in the inappropriately named "Gourmet Ghetto." How a city that prides itself on sensitivity can call one of its wealthiest neighborhoods a ghetto, while to the south real zones of impoverishment stretch toward Oakland's notoriously less well-off streets, remains a mystery that soy lattes in cups of recycled cardboard can't explain. I work at an elementary school here, a moderately employed after-school drone. The kids that entertain me maintain certain characteristics childhood teaches, but I can't understand their progenitors. In Berkeley, bumper stickers abound; desperate for recognition, left-wingers soothe guilt by advertising disapproval of the government, oil companies, farmed salmon, school vouchers. Berkeley recently voted to impeach President Bush. What importance this smug gesture—apparently, part of a larger claim (cultural and political superiority)—has to the rest of the world remains unclear. Regardless, it too strikes me as a sign that the political sophistication, the self-satisfied, so-called liberal outlook that Berkley residents manage both to share, and to struggle over, endlessly—serves as insufficient drapery for the adolescent life-styles that residents ask one another to overlook. Every adult of a certain age and political persuasion has a story about Berkeley. These recycled narratives grate on me. Remnant of changes that The Sixties failed to bring, Berkeley stands as hippiedom's last outpost, reminder that conservatism remains America's fore-most product: manufacturer of excess, trimmer of the world's flesh, enforcer of fear. Once inside the valley of Hinnom called Berkeley, two forces define daily life: wealth and poverty. The liquor store can't match the Whole Foods shopping experience, but if you don't have a car or the time to make your way across town, the products lining its shelves will fill bellies. Sergeant Pepper, I care about politics, but I don't think a few vegetarian meals make things better, I don't think my own progressive beliefs make things better, I don't always buy organic, I don't always recycle. I confess my shortcomings to you because I know you understand failure, you understand politics as a personal obligation to criticize without regret. You offer your own identity as a shelter for those of us stranded by political indecencies. I should clarify: when I say politics, I mean something specific, something like a blue military jacket's shiny brass button, but this something always changes. When I say politics, I mean something you can lose after a few trips through the washing machine. Composting my coffee grinds, I pledge my devotion to human waste. I'm hedging my bets. If the revolution comes before I die, I hope it kills me.

To revolution; if not revolution, to impending environmental catastrophes that sunsets remake as beauty.

Ramsey

Dear Sergeant Pepper,

Tonight I think about flowers, and because I don't know anything about them, I plan to make my dispatch brief. Flowers, like historical facts and geographical details, become measures of learning: tidbits thrown as conversation pieces wherein speakers declare a certain knowledge. I avoid poetry about flowers; too often, I can't imagine the actual blossom to which the poet refers. I think what I mean to say concerning flowers is that ignorance remains a value I can't do without, something

I find has its own rewards. In ignorance I find a curative for elitism, that which defines the sector of humanity that draws my malaise. The Beatles don't interest me. I don't have time to gather the facts that fandom requires. I have the time, but not the interest. Perhaps I have a little interest, and a little time, but not enough time or interest. I think The Beatles end for me when I see Paul singing in the middle of the Super Bowl. Commercial reality crushes countercultural myth. You, like your progenitors, grow small under the shadow cast by capitalism's great silhouette. Perhaps that's where I take my interest: standing in the same shadow, I feel the communal swoon your wealth wrings from onlookers. We wait for wealth to awe us, we shudder with wonder at the great accumulations others amass, amazed that labors we contribute disappear and then reemerge as somebody else's megamillions. Flowers, like rock bands, serve as ornaments for wedding receptions. What I want to remember about you marries carnation to incantation, evanesces when pigments become chants that monks make over candlewax.

Ramsey

Dear Sergeant Pepper,

I'd like to crown couches in an essay dedicated to the cushioned nature of their beings. Monarchs of the domestic, couches ground family life. Let's toast to televised excess and commercial indulgence. Your music feeds adolescent cravings, croons to soccer moms whose desire for countercultural authenticity can't get beyond nostalgia's pop outcroppings. What do I know of your progenitors, The Beatles? The Sergeant Pepper I imagine amalgamates John and Paul, but leaves room for George and Ringo. Listening to my parents' records, I counted knots in the wooden ceiling while lying upside down, the couch my correspondent. To this day I can't dance. I blame The Beatles for my choreographic shortcomings. In my unmusical upbringing The Beatles take the place commas assume in these letters: they interrupt, but allow for further error. I write to you because your unoccupied body signals the blank sign The Sixties never occupy, an emptiness where history abandons me to musical pleasure. And what accompanies this pleasure? My sense that The Sixties, like the concept album that bears your name, go unfinished. Idealism swallowed whole by capitalism's boundless appropriative apparatuses, the Sixties consume hope. Just visit Berkeley; you'll see that domesticity reforms radicalism according to tricks of the market. The stroller converts sit-in sites, remakes them as avenues for family performances in which couples take turns playing the disgruntled spouse. In truth, I ache for your return, but my cynicism, coached by your disappearance, re-emerges when I see upper-middle class children group-singing Beatles songs for school pageants. "Yellow Submarine" has traded psychedelic undertones for sophomoric innocence; I blame you. In your absence, idiocy becomes our most profound product. In Berkeley, adults claim superiority, convinced that personal political awareness transcends America's global ignorance; amidst well-heeled liberals, I find my nostalgia for idealistic earth-enthusiasts sapped by post-Sixties flakiness that yoga dupes and hibiscus tea-sipping hybrid-driving soul-searching middle-aged divorce lawyers epitomize. Everyone has a cause, but no one's going to sacrifice anything, myself included. I'm going back to sleep, but not to the soothing sounds of your music, which remind me that movements—like pop music—become useful refrains when taking action seems like too much of a risk.

Let's meet in Yalta; from its mountainous coastline we'll carve our own versions of twentieth-century history.

Ramsey

Dear Sergeant Pepper,

I think of you when I clip my toenails; "That's the present," I say, "leftover deposits the body converts into protective coverings." In my effort to purge myself of the reminiscences your music conjures, I read Sei Shonagon's *Pillow Book*. Walking to work, I think of the dirty nun who sings outside the Empress's room, waiting for some food or small favor. Growing up in Oregon, I fashioned the remnants of the commune that once populated the forest near our house into the ruins of early European settlers. A half-built log cabin became, for me, a pioneer's makeshift shelter. Perhaps ruins contradict their own histories, become timeless as the chronological orders that begat them crumble and rot in forgotten mezzanines. Parents teach history as the glitches that interrupt recording technologies. When the video camera fails or the digital camera malfunctions, history emerges as the undocumented. Family histories use the past to account for current inadequacies; my pillbox empty, I turn pedestrian and walk toward sobriety. I'd like to own a mattock and spend days chopping up soil for seeds I don't own. That's how I understand labor. Effort expended without purpose. Childbirth must be something else, Matterhorn to my mattock. At a party given by friends of my parents, a bearded guru asked me what animal I'd like to be. I must have been about six. His attitude exuded child-speak expertise, as though I ought to appreciate his ability to speak down to me. A dog, I said, refusing to elaborate, but thinking of my family pet's ability to run, sleep, eat. The guru said he'd like to be a bird, and blabbered about soaring, eyesight, hawks, wind. I think this exchange condenses what I don't like about your generation: you understand ornithological traits as superior to canine practicalities. My parents' friends owned lamas. They encouraged potluck sensibilities, but fed idealism to inbred Labrador retrievers.

If these letters arrange themselves like leaves, let orthostichy guide their arrangement.

Ramsey

Dear Sergeant Pepper,

Today I listen to your *Lonely Hearts Club Band*, thinking of the Bhagwan Rajneesh. As the cult leader of my youth, he hood-winked fellow Oregonians eager for mystical guidance; his followers briefly established an ill-fated commune that collapsed in 1985, just a few years after its founding. That same year, the Bhagwan was deported. I grew up around classmates whose parents traded Ken Kesey novels for the Good Book. Born-again

Christians may be rare in Berkeley, but the faith with which residents pursue shiitake mushrooms suggests that idealists grow old as gourmands, transcending earthly concerns in moments of culinary bliss. At the corner store, I purchase frozen corn dogs, my wife's current craving. Outside, drug dealers' cigarettes bob and weave, mapping ritual movements. A poster advertising exterminators invokes termites. Back at work, giggling students ask if I'm a hippie. This noun conjures style, artifice. On the way home from work I stop at Berkeley Bowl, a grocery store with progressive trappings, but I can't get through the logjam they call the bulk food isle. I head home, empty-handed. What kind of parent do you think I'll become? A red, flowered, corduroy bag my wife calls the *dad bag* holds books that don't fit in my backpack. "Only a dad can be seen carrying such a bag," she says, explaining her nomenclature. Still, I've used this bag for several years now; a student of mine at Brooklyn College once told me the dad bag demonstrated, as he put it, a confident masculinity. I'm not a dad yet, but I carry the bag. Perhaps I'll be a dad like Al Morse, childhood neighbor, a born-again who raised his kids on *Rambo* movies and re-runs of *The A-Team*. Sergeant Pepper, what role do you play in these entertainment extravaganzas, propaganda (should I say morality?) tales in which men emasculated by Vietnam regain their spunk through courageous acts of violence. My friend Silas, son of former hippie Al, eschewed evolution for creationism, though he excelled at science; last I heard he was studying neurobiology somewhere down South. Perhaps the willful ignorance of the researcher is the scientific equivalent of the soldier who pursues what they call bravery in a battle against impossible odds. Rather than soldiery, I prefer an *olla podrida* of intoxication, insubordination and molestation, a melodramatic defenestration of *Das Kapital*. My childhood dictionary exhibits four varieties of the mechanical nut: hexagonal, wing, square, cap. One is circled. Can you guess which?

Ramsey

Dear Sergeant Pepper,

Remember Rhodesia, Burma, Abyssinia, Kampuchea? A Sergeant like yourself should respect former names as ciphers for remote operations. My grandmother brought me maracas after a trip to Guadalajara. Was this gesture meant to communicate in a code I never understood? Rhythmically underprivileged, I used my maracas as paddles and swatted Nerf balls around the living room, careful not to target the record player, my parents' finest appliance. George (my father) showing me how to clean records: a recollection that fails to account for technology's supposed aversion to nostalgia. What forms of outdated knowledge will I provide for my children? We light our menorah, but can't remember the proper prayer. No matter; religion is, for us, mescaline in vodka, or the miracle we comprehend when, at last, the coffee brews. God? We write that topic off as the proper toxin for meshugganas.

I write from bed, contemplating F.A. Mesmer to avoid Freud; thanks for listening,

Ramsey

Dear Sergeant Pepper,

My brother's recipe for opium tea leaves me almost euphoric, incredibly constipated. For a long time now I've been thinking of the word "onus." To me, it doesn't signify duty or responsibility; it points sideways, to "anus." As a child, I believed anus was a name, like Amos. I had to remind myself of the difference constantly, like reminding myself to say "kernel" when I read "colonel." In the newspaper today, a Berkeley resident (who, the paper suggests, "earned his lefty stripes" during years of public school teaching) rails against the homelessness that interrupts his ride through town in his new convertible. In high school, I wrote letters for Amnesty International and imagined firebombing national guard outposts; have I too earned the right to abandon my politics for material indulgence? Shall we reserve this right for Baby Boomers alone? I'm blending my yogurt with painkillers. I plan to nap my way toward fatherhood. I don't want tickets to Ravi Shankar, I don't want freshly squeezed organic orange juice. I'm thinking of the Sixties when I stir my coffee, but it's a valentine I most desire, signed by you.

Take your time; the tea I pour makes the window's mullions tremble.

Ramsey

Dear Sergeant Pepper,

Abbreviating a phone conversation, I announce my constipation with conviction. In the silence that ensues, I contemplate digestion as *tekhne*. Still high—but not from the opium tea—I organize tomato sauces the cabinet can't hold. The pyramid I construct pinnacles Bolognese. A local kennel's logo claims that "It Takes a Village to Raise a Pet." I feed the remainder of my leukemogenic frankfurter to the family dog, thinking of facts from the *Science Times*. Yesterday we woke to frost, Berkeley frozen over, an aberrant weather pattern descending. In the book I'm reading for the dissertation I don't feel like writing, "inextricably linked" appears, a phrase my teacher once flagged in my own writing, citing general overuse. The author asserts autobiography as political protest, while I envision the local diner's *plat du jour*. These sentences trace Sei Shonagon's subject, "people who look pleased with themselves"; I leave it to you to decide who's who. Meanwhile, let's recollect collaboration as one legacy of the Sixties, still visible when teachers, claiming progressive values, force students to participate in group projects. In my childhood Reagan presided. The *Lonely Hearts Club Band* played countermelodies to Eighties excess, but seven years into the presidency of George W. Bush, discord reigns. I still hear your group, but when I reach for my ideals I'm Tantalus, neck-deep in somebody's unsavory soup.

Let this last letter commemorate transsexuality, Nancy Reagan's unacknowledged mentor.

Ramsey

DEAR ██████████████████

Dear ████████████,

Thank you very much for your thoughtful rejection; I really, truly appreciate your response. Please accept my apologies in advance for what follows, as I know you probably have neither the time nor the inclination to hear my thoughts, most of which concern the reader's report I received regarding "Theaters of Desire: Samuel R. Delany's Anecdotal Tricks."

I cannot, for reasons that you clearly recognize, change the essay to appeal to specific varieties of academic discourse, as championed by your reader. To put my reservations into academic jargon: the empty, hegemonic rhetoric of "critique" and "argument" is nothing less than a gatekeeping mechanism that helps to control what can or cannot be included within so-called scholarly discourse.

In this regard, I am also appreciative of your reader's frustration with the "jarring" effects of my essay; it's not, like, by accident. The reader's valorization of conventional academic forms—of "structured, organized way[s] of examining" subjects—is not an innocent, objective standard; it is, on the contrary, another manifestation of exclusionary practices that inform academic hierarchies, and that have long been used in the "policing of certain forms of sexual and racial identity."

I'm reminded of my experiences working at a nightclub many years ago. "You can invite all the gay boys you want," the promoter told us, "but what we really want is the ones who look straight."

Unfortunately, even when it espouses a "queer of color critique" (for example), the closely guarded perimeter that defines academic discourse reconstructs certain all-too-familiar political dynamics—the very same dynamics according to which supposedly unquestionable "values" ultimately reinforce inequalities according to differences of race, class, gender, sexual orientation, etc., etc. In many cases, the insistence that a given project include this or that thinker who has previously discussed related topics, or whose work might "complicate" or "problematize" the subject of a given inquiry strikes me as a particularly useful ruse. Too often, "joining the conversation" means looking at things the way others do—with minor, "well-argued," "well-organized" differences, of course.

Although Samuel R. Delany is indeed a part of "queer of color critique," and of queer theory more broadly conceived, he never received the institutionalized training, and has never really occupied the same professional and institutional positions as many MLA-sanctioned "experts" in the field, whose uses of anecdote (in most cases aggressively employed, I might add, only after these experts have proven themselves by displaying more conventional academic chops) better conform to so-called professional standards—including your reader's preferred example, my former professor (may she rest in peace), Eve Sedgwick.

(Incidentally, your reader's suggestion that I examine the work of another former professor of mine, my friend and mentor Robert Reid-Pharr, strikes me as an especially precious proposition. The essay I submitted to you began as a paper for a class Robert taught on Samuel R. Delany, and was first delivered at a conference on Delany at SUNY Buffalo. Mr. Delany was in attendance, and while one should never assume that a writer can fairly judge criticism about his work, Chip, as he prefers to be called, enthusiastically approved of my project.)

At any rate, reducing Samuel R. Delany's use of anecdotes to a "theoretical strategy," one that might be placed in the same category as the comparatively staid versions of anecdotal writings suggested by your reader, conveniently ignores Delany's insistence upon contaminating discourses in order to be "jarring"; "jarring" might be, in some cases, a practical (as much as it might also be a theoretical) device.

Anecdotes that are circumcised, or circumscribed, or otherwise excised, anecdotes that thus might more easily slip into the carefully guarded dress worn by academic discourse—such anecdotes may have their uses, but such uses do not, in my view, do credit to Delany's use of anecdotes. In this regard, my essay is also an homage of sorts, and perhaps, seen from this angle, it exceeds its purpose. After all, I should know that gestures of reverence ought not so freely voice themselves in academic discourse—and when they do, they should be politely expressed in, for example, the acknowledgements page of one's book—and if such mentions do not show the depths of one's appreciation, they might at least provide some opportunity for future career advancements.

Lastly, the deployment of "jarring" practices is not at all "experimental" (your reader's term for my work—a familiar term, and a damning one, used to dismiss so many queer writings!). It is, on the contrary, a strategy developed as part and parcel of many critiques that recognize, in the beast of conventions and forms and "scholarly rigor," the spawn of conservative ideologies long-dominant—and perhaps hardly worth challenging, at this point—but ideologies that I would prefer to critique, nonetheless.

In light of the continuing insistence upon conventionality and mindless "professionalization" within the academy, despite whatever headway so many well-argued critiques have made against the seemingly inherent benefits of "organization," "rationalism," "groupthink," etc., the occasional foray into formal disobedience seems to me a justifiable response.

Once again, thank you so very much for your thoughtful rejection, for pursuing a reader, and for reading, if you have been able to, my own thoughts on the matters at hand.

If you get the inclination to put together an issue on the ways that formal conventions contain, constrict, and control academic discourse, let me know—as you can see, it's a topic I've been thinking about for some time.

Sincerely,

Ramsey Scott

THEATERS OF DESIRE:
SAMUEL R. DELANY'S ANECDOTAL TRICKS

"Here's how it happens"—I've always wanted to say that to open an essay.

Or, something like, "Okay, let me give it to you straight…"

Or, "The truth is…"

A direct rhetorical thrust of a sentence: that's exactly what I'd like to give, but can't. I'm more comfortable mixing my metaphors, chasing the cut-ups I call theory.

I'd like to profess, but in this case what I want to profess has nothing to do with the responsibility of a public declaration; called to account for his expertise, a professional or a professor professes, announces a devotion of sorts, claims a knowledge or skill. I'm thinking instead of the anecdote, the epitome of un-scientific evidence, least professional of all discourses, the mode through which the writer lances the impersonality of theory and declares her allegiance to first-hand experience.

I have an observation: Samuel R. Delany's discourse shelters anecdote. Ungovernable, the anecdote seeps into cracks discourse would like to seal with what others call methodology, logic, analytical reasoning, philosophical cunning. It countenances the wink, its physiognomic equivalent. If I could make my method scientific, my observations would proceed toward hypotheses, predictions, experiments, conclusions...but when I think of science, I recollect sneaking out of my eighth grade biology class with my textbook and masturbating to the image of the fetal pig.

Nobody's discourse is a lynchpin for logic.

I would like to proceed by observation and hypothesis, but leave out the experiment and conclusion I reached in the third stall of the Boys' Room at Hanby Junior High. If the essay I write can be a sanctuary, let it safeguard the sentences that won't order its proper outcome, let the essay become an affirmation of the thesis I can't provide, let it announce my failure to be professional. Every sanctuary, like discourse, consents to what it omits. You can't fit a full crate of lemons into your hatband. The anecdote my alibi, I abjure argument in favor of the seepage Delany's essays introduce as reminiscences and recollections, short voyages into narrative that never leave the shore.

The difficulty for me in discussing Delany is that his writing produces and consumes its own commentary. There are derivations and diversions of discourse, partially built into his texts and perhaps also products of my own misreadings. Take *The Fall of the Towers*, a book in which there's no war but the one they brainwash into the heads of the soldiers, sure it's science I guess, science fiction they say, but I read that book and to me there's almost no fiction; or "The Tale of Plagues and Carnivals," you're in the fantasy land Delany creates in his Nevèrÿon series, then New York and the AIDS epidemic, submersed in a narrative that ingests its own paratexts along with its supposed critics, its K. Leslie Steiners and S.L. Kermits…[40] a genre like the academic essay or the science fiction novel cannot endure, it's a protected area and you can pass in and out, but it's got its own guards and like airport security their only job is to prevent certain things from getting through the gate. You can try to hack your way through with an axe or hatchet, and at the gate they go straight for your shoes, you take them off and when they come out the other end of the x-ray machine your hatchet's in your pocket and it's Delany's story, "The Tale of Plagues and Carnivals." "The law of discourses, like the law of genres," Delany writes, "is that 'Discourses are not mixed'… As with the law of genres, the truth of the law is that it can never be obeyed: like genres, discourses never arrive pure."[41]

This essay concerns anecdote, but its purpose is meaner, more precise: to puncture the indefatigable comfort the academic finds in the essay as vessel for knowledge, as testament to research, as scaffolding for argument. Consider the following digression concerning an encounter in the now defunct Cameo theater as it appears in Delany's essay, "Aversion, Perversion, Diversion":

> As we began to touch each other, he leaned toward me to whisper, in a light, working-class accent associated with the outlying boroughs of the city, "You know, I've never done anything like this before. All the other sex I've had has been with women. But somebody told me about this place. So I just thought…" He shrugged. And we continued, easily enough considering his virgin status, to some satisfaction for us both.

Three months later, visiting the theater once more, after a stroll down one aisle and up the other, I noticed the same young man, again sitting off on one side. Recalling our last encounter, I slid in immediately to sit a seat away from him, smiled, and said softly, "Hi!" This time, he motioned me to the next seat right away, grinning and saying hello. As we began to touch each other, again he bent forward to explain: "You know, I've never done anything like this before—with a man, I mean. I've had sex with women, sure. But this is my first time doing it with a guy..."[42]

This anecdote frames my project; what gets repeated in the darkness of the theater provides the investigatory limits of my own essay. Regarding his encounters with this perpetual first-timer, Delany asks a number of questions concerning the man's erotic interests, the possibility that this rhetorical frame of feigned virginity functions as his "portable closet," the social constraints that might have coerced him into adopting it as his strategy for seduction, the Freudian reading ("repetition is desire") implicit in his behavior. Questions brush up against storytelling; evidence, anecdotal, suggests answers left incomplete.

From the history of demolished theaters, desire stirs its own stories, preserved in Delany's essays, resistant to the dismantling discourse demands. "Discourse," Delany writes, "is what tells us what is central and what is peripheral—what is a mistake, an anomaly, an accident, a joke."[43] Mistakes, anomalies, jokes: these figures, fuel for anecdote, inform the measure I want to take against the essay that arrives chained to discourse, driven toward certain conclusions, strung up on what others call *scholarship* and *rigor*. Delany as my guide, I want the theater of the essay wrenched free from discourse's grip; defiled by anecdote, the essay I want to write degrades itself.

If I accept as my margin of error some fraction of, or addition to, the distance between, say, Hackensack and Paterson, I may be closer to what remains unfocused: I'd like to interrogate Delany's habitual slippage into anecdotal narrative. I say habitual because, if it is true that, as Foucault has written, "we cannot simply speak of anything, when we like or where we like; not just anyone, finally, may speak of just anything," it is also true that anyone, or almost anyone, can tell a story.[44]

Hypothesis: The story maintains a position above and below critical discourse, the story is top and bottom, the story is versatile, a supposedly primitive predecessor to theory and the object of its critical gaze, remembered, dismembered. As such, the story also slips through my discourse. If these propositions appear as notices pinned to corkboards, let them announce, like drug trials, the need for human subjects; let them depict, like snapshots photocopied into faintness, half-gestures toward the scientific principles I haven't the wherewithal to enact.

I want to notice Delany's essays in which he's got a topic like language or discourse or the public policy of disinformation on sex and he's giving it to you, the reader, like a Gibson, I mean the martini with onions, and every onion becomes anecdote, inside the onions there's a movie theater, it's 1983, there's a guy giving somebody a blow job and you practically tear up trying to keep reading because it's a strong onion and you can't drink enough discourse to get the guy's wet-lipped grin out of your mind. Delany writes:

While I sat in the balcony of the Variety Photoplays Theater in New York, a tall, muscular white man in his mid-thirties, in combat boots, Air Force flight jacket, with a military crew, finished sucking off one black guy in a paint-stained jacket, only to climb over the back of the seats of the row between us and, steadying himself on my shoulder, grinned at me with the wet-lipped delight of the satisfied. I grinned back, but felt constrained to say, softly, to this stranger who, until a minute before, had only been a head bobbing up and down between the legs of the man in the row in front of me, "Aren't you worried about AIDS?"

Here I would like to suggest that what gets whispered to strangers in the darkness of the theater is what gets lost, goes missing, can't factor as data in the kind of critical study I refuse to undertake.

"Aren't you worried about AIDS?"

"Naw," [says the grinning man to Delany,] "You can't get it sucking dick—unless you got cuts in your mouth or something like that." [45]

An anecdote like this one sticks to things, it's like spaghetti, if properly cooked, the next thing you know you're peeling it off the walls. "Dinner's ready!" If my ideas seem overcooked it's because I've seen theaters in my spaghetti, anecdotes I read in Delany's critical essays. Think of the anecdote as a gift for the reader, one she doesn't know how to accept. It's not fact after all, it's not entirely hers (it comes from the purported experience of another), but under its shelter she observes what otherwise goes unwitnessed.

Hypothesis: The anecdote needles its way into discourse, threads together the scientific and the social; the anecdote leaves no seams. Outlined by desire, ejaculated in essay's theaters, anecdote splatters on the toilet seat of the real. "Art and science," writes Muriel Rukeyser, "have investigated each other from the beginning... both... are languages ready to be betrayed in translation; but their roots spread through our tissue, their deepest meanings fertilize us, and reaching our consciousness, they reach each other."[46] Replace science with discourse, art with anecdote; recollect the Greek antecedent to our anecdote, *anekdota*, things unpublished. In Delany's essays, anecdotes frequently engage the fringes of experience, where experiments with desire and sexuality lead toward the almost secret sanctuaries outside the page, sanctuaries readers construct for themselves.

If I could write an essay in language wiped clean of its cobwebs, immunized against contamination, I would not choose the anecdote to deliver my argument. Capitalized, Anecdote only signals its own insufficient capital. What I want to capitalize is not the notion of infection or contamination—the anecdote doesn't really infect *or* contaminate—its method is seductive, its progress tethered to intrigue, its epistemology defined by entitlement. The opportunity to listen to an anecdote signals privilege. And yet its form remains egalitarian, its methodology insistent upon storytelling as the guide to knowledge. No sentence arrives unblemished by language's imperfections. Perhaps the anecdote is only another accessory to the lavish outfits language already dons. The provenance of the anecdote can't be chronicled; its record of ownership maps diversity itself, catalogues a discursive elasticity that so-called *research methodologies* and other forms of academic fantasy try to forget.

At some previous moment in the anecdote's history, someone must have already asked what role desire plays amidst storytelling. Why not link desire to anecdote? The science of statistics dismisses anecdote out of hand. In the essay, autobiographical, anecdotal evidence roots the speaker as subject, the author's authority as indefatigable presence. I want to think of the anecdote as a signal, a reminder: the difference between storytelling and professional, academic discourse can't be found in language. I want to recapitulate, following Delany, the essay as anecdote's future retreat. Desire my guide, I want to essay an understanding of anecdote as Delany's peculiar innovation. From his position as a writer with a reputation established outside the academy, gracing its margins as an itinerant professor, Delany peeks in on scholarly arguments, but constructs essays that refuse the terms academic writing requires.

His marginal existence astride the boundaries of academic discourse raises questions concerning the policing of professional, scholarly writing. Recently, the supposed return of rigor through scientific, historically based research suggests a shelving of the arguments Derrida (for example) constructs regarding the permeability of language, its endless retreat into metaphor, the hemorrhaging of discourses that constantly handcuffs the most carefully constructed philosophical or scientific argument. The slippage into anecdote that occurs in Delany's essays signals a further provocation; it introduces the author as underground traveler, one whose experiences bridge the division between the scholarly and the abject, the criminal—what Freud would label perverse.

At the gates of the academy, I wonder whether its halls may actually shelter Freud's perverts, whether travelers of the underground can use it as retreat in exchange for salacious tales.

What about accountability? Remember that the hero of Delany's most well-known novel, *Dalgren*, begins his travels without a name, enters the city to experience its vices without identity.[47] A professional identity is a sheen, a screen, a process of disidentification. To transgress the conventions of professional conduct and academic discourse—to present oneself, in one's own writing, as irresponsible, disobedient, and unprofessional—punctures that screen, reminds us that it is not impermeable, but is, in fact, constructed. Within the academy, the possible projects that count as work remain carefully controlled. Academic writing demands a purification of discourse, as if language might be sterilized. In Delany's essays, the anecdote suggests otherwise. For Delany, the anecdote is the organ that dilates the orifice known as language.

And what of anecdote, as seen by the anthropologist Kathleen Stewart: "What if I tried to arrest the progress of truth claims that reduce 'anecdotal evidence' to a secondary and deeply suspect status?" writes Stewart. "What if I tried to invert the hierarchy of 'conceptual thought' over 'data' and to take my own task of cultural translation as the supplement? What if in the place of a transcendent system or code there was only the anecdote, the fragment—insufficient and unfinished?"[48]

The anecdote as a challenge to data drives Delany's essay "Street Talk/Straight Talk," in which the informal confidentiality in conversations about sex between near strangers interrupts discourse concerning the spread of AIDS. Witnessing the process through which publicly sponsored pronouncements exaggerating the danger of this disease contribute to constraints against all forms of public sex, regardless of the relative risk levels attributable to specific behaviors, Delany calls into question the mechanism by which science is utilized to enforce limitations on freedom. "Are we speaking," writes Delany, "of something that can, if one wishes, be simply called the scientific method? No. We are speaking, rather, of what happens to such a 'method' in a field ripe with and riddled by despair and terror and prior political agendas that flagrantly, at all levels, abnegate that method."[49]

The anecdote is personal, but its armature connects the teller, first-person protagonist, to history. The conditions of the anecdote bespeak this provisional existence inside time's itinerant theater: speaking from experience, the storyteller casts a backward glance; the anecdote is a *fort/da* device, its movement conditioned by repetition, in which the teller recapitulates what otherwise vanishes in the void others call forgetting. Benjamin, writing of the decline of storytelling in his famous essay on the subject, proposes that "it is possible to see a new beauty in what is vanishing."[50] Like Benjamin, Delany bears witness to the enclaves eclipsed by history. His testimonies concerning these spaces speak to pressures, economic and social, political and symbolic, that break the mystique of the *demimonde*, that colonize and commodify previously unacknowledged spaces where transgression writes its own permits.

The authority for occupation stems from discursive regimes that privilege protection over freedom, public health over private pleasure, rigorous argument over anecdotal or experiential evidence.

As the behavior of the individual encounters the ever-novel surveillance systems organized by the state, personal testimony from the underground traveler gains new credence: to profess what others call perverse, to identify with the marginalized, to proclaim the value in spaces others consider insignificant... These actions represent not only a rejection of discursive regimes that restrict language; they also suggest a willingness on the part of the author to account for his own work as valuable, and to align himself against those who would champion the state's rigid boundaries, its laws designed to intimidate, disenfranchise, stratify, alienate.

I want to perform my own interrogation, one that quivers in anticipation of an aesthetic pleasure. In the movie theaters that serve as shelters for secretive intercourse and that Delany revisits in his essays, aesthetic pleasure seems secondary; gratification names the first prerogative, usually sexual, though the boundary of sexual pleasure encompasses a range of behaviors so large that identifying a given act as sexual depends as much on the spectator as the actors. Although sexual gratification once drew men (and perhaps, as Delany claims, some women) to the theaters, Delany also suggests that the theaters allowed interracial, interclass "contact" on a level not possible in other social spaces. It is this contact that provides the highest possible benefits: "Given the mode of capitalism under which we all live, life is at its most rewarding, productive, and pleasant when large numbers of people understand, appreciate, and seek out interclass contact and communication conducted in a mode of good will."[51]

I believe the genius of the anecdote has everything to do with the potential for such a "rewarding, productive, pleasant" life.

The theaters allow for the contact described above; in so doing, they also recast desire's products as a frontier, an endless array of behaviors for which no complete survey exists, behaviors that evade the expectations of the participants themselves, that flicker and effloresce amidst exceptional, otherwise antisocial acts. The anecdote, connoisseur of the exceptional, is the theater of desire's most able chronicler, capturing in its brevity the momentary recognition strangers grant one another in an instant of sexual bliss.

Observation: Nostalgia (if Delany's essays contain nostalgia)—utopian milieus (if the theater can be seen as one such utopia)—the aestheticization of antisocial behavior (but doesn't this aestheticization exist already, deeply imbedded in the culture Delany both harnesses and scrutinizes—namely, commercialized, corporatized America?)—amidst these attributes, Delany's essays offer safe passage, provide openings and invitations, serve as means of conjuring. In the dilation of discourse by anecdote, his essays provide the stage for desire to reshape social space.

Hypothesis: Delany's anecdotes explore conflicts engendered by orifices and obstructions, patterns and variations—all the mechanisms of rule-making and rule-breaking that divert desire's flows across the body of the text, that give shape to discourse.

Observation: The rupture of the border between the academic and the pornographic, the personal and the public, between fiction and non-fiction, light and dark—the listing of dichotomies—the continual demand to order and disorder—these things I cite in order to avoid saying I've become lost inside the anecdotes I meant to investigate.[52]

Hypothesis: If I want to address the anecdotal function as it appears in Delany's essays I must first consider the opening into which my thoughts slip, the opening in the following anecdote concerning the now defunct Variety Photoplays Theater, as described in Delany's *Times Square Red, Times Square Blue*. After witnessing a young man masturbate repeatedly before a shifting group of self-stimulating onlookers, Delany is in the lobby when, he writes, "I looked away from the ticket taker arguing on his stool with his two friends, up the stairway to the balcony... the same young man ambled lackadaisically down. I saw—with some shock—his fly was open. His uncut penis, along with both testicles, hung free."[53] It's this flapping fly into which my thoughts slip, out of which genitals flop. It's where I enter the essay; the genial climate to which my experiments desire access begins at its edges, hypotheses bleached on the laundry line I want to call history.

Hypothesis: If my hypothesis suggests that I need to examine this flapping fly in order to understand the anecdotal function at work in Delany's essays, testing my hypothesis would require me to ignore this opening, to re-center my efforts elsewhere; if I get nowhere, it's because my thoughts remain trapped in the once-opened fly that closes when the young man, after having been threatened with removal by the staff of the theater, "finally, pushe[s] his privates back in his slacks."[54]

Observation: The fly and the lobby function analogously, as if to fence and delimit desire—although, as Frank O'Hara says in "Digression on 'Number 1,' 1948," "They'll / never fence the silver range."[55] I like to imagine that the silver range encompasses movies, desire, transgression. "Mothers of America / let your kids go to the movies!" O'Hara writes. "They may even be grateful to you / for their first sexual experience."[56]

In Joe LeSueur's memoir, *Digressions on Some Poems by Frank O'Hara,* the anecdote fosters its own sort of methodology, however erratic and ungovernable. LeSueur's anecdotes revel in the uncouth behavior of friends, lovers, and acquaintances; anecdotes drive his narrative, or derail it, or both, all at once. In his cinematic retelling of an argument between Frank O'Hara and Lee Krasner, LeSueur watches, reclining on a beach towel, as Frank goes to talk to Lee. Suddenly, LeSueur writes, Krasner "unleashes what is clearly a barrage of angry words; it causes Frank to flinch, as indeed I do, watching the scene unfold, trying without success to catch what she's saying."[57] This flinch records the anecdotal reflex, instant of recognition, wherein history sticks to narrative's pliant physiognomy. "The kid watched the movie a few more minutes," Delany writes of yet another moviegoer, until "finally he pushed his cock back into his jeans and zipped up."[58] When the fly is zipped, discourse smoothes the wrinkles out of its slacks, dreams new zippers, for every limb its own zipper, a zipper for every orifice, a sacrificial zipper, a zipper for each finger; the zipper refashions discourse into sartorial metaphor.

If discourse zips, the anecdote unzips. Consider, for example, LeSueur's retelling of the anecdotal stylings of W.H. Auden's friend and lover, the poet Chester Kallman:

> Those of us who caught his act—Frank [O'Hara], John Button, and I, plus two or three other San Remo regulars—listened in consternation as he went on and on about some georgeous,

extravagantly hung hustler he'd brought home just the other night to the St. Mark's Place flat he shared with W.H. Auden, and how Wystan, awakened by the goings-on, called out, "Chester! Is that you?" and how Chester, unwillingly disengaging himself from the giant phallus he was devouring, answered, "Yes, Wystan," and immediately went back to doing what he called "the Lord's work," as Wystan now asked, "Ches-ter? Are you alone?" and Chester, again coming up for air, called out, "No, Wystan, go back to sleep"—all of this accompanied by the telling and obscene gestures of Chester's lascivious mouth going down and then coming up, graphically indicating the great length of the hustler's member as well as the great pleasure Chester took in servicing him.[59]

LeSueur claims that, in reaction to Kallman's performances, O'Hara decides to change his own behavior, and resolves that he will *not* to act like Chester Kallman: "I'd noticed that Frank no longer engaged in wild sexual exploits—like, for example, his regularly making out with the guard at the U.N. during its construction… or like the time he boarded the subway, blind drunk, missed his stop and ended up in Queens, where he blew the Negro in the change booth before catching his train back to Manhattan."[60] LeSueur's text delights in layers of anecdotal retelling; the anecdote of O'Hara's resolution *not* to engage in "wild sexual exploits" thus provides the opportunity to mention, in passing, various acts of that very nature.

If Joe LeSueur's recollections do not take the form of essays, *per se*, let me analyze by misidentification in order to further my own project. If I can't be Chester Kallman or the hustler he brings back, let me note instead that an anecdote retold to the proper audience can refashion otherwise ignominious incidents as heroic acts, acts worth remembering. In the digressions I want to call LeSeur's essays, anecdotes constitute evidence for writing's mystery. They don't explain poetry, just as Delany's movie theater encounters don't explain desire. Instead, LeSeur and Delany construct, anecdotally, a model poetry desires: real events reduced to a simple unzip, a flinch.

Hypothesis: The combination of discourse and anecdote inflames the reader of the essay; the smoke into which her thoughts pass asphyxiates critical passages like the noose around the neck of an autoerotic self-strangulator; where the author enters discourse disperses and the body revives in the iron lung the anecdote supplies; thusly does desire's narrative ignite in the brick fireplace known as the essay. "There are as many different styles, intensities, and timbres to sex as there are people," Delany writes after his encounter with the flapping fly. "The variety and nuance and attitude blends into the variety of techniques and actions employed, which finally segues, as seamlessly, into the variety of sexual objects the range of humankind desires."[61] If desire is the silver range that can't be fenced, discourse stretches, a system of posts and wires, gates and lookouts, across desire's range. This range can't be mapped, its locus is everywhere and nowhere, its coordinates insufficient. The possible positions and movements of the bodies that occupy its expanse, those who gather and embrace in secreted locales, can't be fathomed in the systematic translations scholarly inquiry makes of sexual pleasures.

Observation: Such uncircumcised sentences represent my continuing failure to articulate the function of the anecdote. I would like to conceive anecdotal writing as an effort always provisional, as a practice of condolences, consolation for loss. The losses the anecdote reproduces as stunted narratives involve figures like

Mike, the blue sneaker fetishist in Delany's essay "Aversion/ Perversion/Diversion," or Billy, the science fiction-loving hustler in the same essay who recognizes Samuel R. Delany as a famous SF author, the Billy who dies, a few years later, of AIDS. These anecdotes are tombstones in the cemetery of desire. Such tales, Delany announces in the same essay, an essay originally presented as a talk at Rutgers University, "belong to a *range* of sexual occurrences, the vast majority of which have never and can never make their way into language."[62] To *profess* allegiance to this range, to sanction—anecdotally—its extremities, is to offer one's own body as the critical site. The caress science withholds signals the need anecdote fulfills. Once summoned, the art of the anecdote reclaims desire in the body of the essay.

Hypothesis: In the interchange between sexuality as a discursive byproduct and sexuality as captured in a first person anecdote— between sexuality as a textually manufactured topic birthing further discourse and sexuality as a trajectory of beginnings and endings, characters and narrators—another field of sexuality emerges, an extra-linguistic "never-said" that might exist beyond the realm of scientific and autobiographical discourse, beyond narration and beyond the relatable experience of any single individual.

And what of desire? Can we figure its reaches, its limitations? Look, says Delany, what others render abstract in one-liners that leave us grasping after vectors reverberating between self and other, I found inside theaters where prostitutes and construction workers rested under the dappled reflections of Ron Jeremy's backside... if you want the abstraction, first consider the semenophile in "On the Unspeakable," he who enters the theater, offers his services to a crack-addicted prostitute, masturbates, and carefully consumes his own ejaculate. This figure can become fodder for the next theory-hog, but theory can't wipe the semen off his hands or clear his image from the reader's mind. His act sticks, like Delany's essay; its residue conjures the anecdote, lipstick on theory's asscheek. A map of desire works like discourse; it fails to account for marauders that attack from unmarked territories. To understand its terrain, you enter; or rather, already inside, you try and find your way out.

Should desire's reaches thus be chronicled as seemingly endless yet finite, Kant's mathematical sublime, a challenge to reason? Such measurable yet unimaginable reckoning attempts to secure discourse's grip over desire's unmanageable mechanisms, turning away from the abject and grand to the reliability of the formula, the equation, the answerable. On the other hand, championing desire's mystery offers no solution; an encounter with Deleuze and Guattari ought to remind us how carefully capital acts to maximize desire's mystique, to materialize its evanescing vapors while preserving its enigmatic origins.

Here Delany's theater scenes offer another channel, a window into what doesn't get told through any metaphysical rendering or reconstructing of desire as capitalism's favorite narcotic: winnowed to a single shoe type and color, collapsed into a preferred anatomical feature, or prefigured by *sotto voce* confessions from married men who prefer fucking men, the scenes autographed by desire maintain socio-economic and historical particularities that puncture any featureless theorizing about the armature desire activates; like politics, all desire is local.

Localized, historicized, desire inhabits the anecdotal; to learn its mechanisms, take an instance and crystallize its essence in prose.

In Jane Gallop's *Anecdotal Theory*, she writes of the impulse to date the story: "'Half a dozen years ago' and 'Twenty-three years ago,'" writes Gallop. "This classic storytelling gambit situates audience and narrator within a shared present moment in the aftermath of the story to be told. Such a gesture not only alludes to oral storytelling but also proffers the story as having happened, makes a claim to telling not only story but history."[63]

An anecdote is a gift, and as such, custom dictates that one accept. Its authority is given; if I say what happened to me as an aside, with a rhetorical flourish that Delany reminds us allows otherwise unspeakable sentences to be spoken (in this case, the familiar "By the way(s)," or, especially if it is humiliating, embarrassing, or unseemly, a "That reminds me of the time when...," all phrases that signal an anecdotal turn), I prepare the receiver to nod in acknowledgement, if not agreement.[64]

The anecdote's purchase on truth, lubricated by rhetorical tricks, Vaselined to penetrate the most resistant receivers, rests on the personal transaction that a short recollection consummates. The anecdote invites its listeners to traffic in the private encounters of its participants; cousin to gossip, it informs by dissent.

Could there be a scientific study of the anecdote? In fact, the protocols necessary to practice science don't apply to the anecdotal, in which digression rules. The potential for an outcome to be measured fades as the climax slips into the shadow stories enact as moral codes, conditions for completion, fictional irreconcilables.

Is there a discrepancy between Gallop's analysis of academic stories traded between scholars and Delany's anecdotes of illicit sex inside 42nd Street theaters? "As soon as there is a question," writes Maurice Blanchot, "there is no reply that could exhaust that question."[65]

I'm not writing to answer questions, I'm not theorizing to propose a theory, I'm not fragmenting my sentences in order to frame the fragment. I'm addressing anecdote because, like the motivation behind the anecdote itself, my motives remain ulterior.

Jane Gallop quotes Joel Fineman's "History of the Anecdote"; I quote Jane Gallop quoting Fineman on the anecdote, that which "'introduces an opening into the teleological... narration of beginning, middle, and end."[66] Gallop suggests anecdotal theory can be "a circuit that passes through different individuals, exchanging anecdotes and theory, in writing but also in the flesh."[67]

Circulation through anecdote undermines official apparatuses, erodes the authority vested in administrative mouthpieces, fosters a community of thinkers outside the sanctioned bodies of the university. But the anecdote also fictionalizes the author-as-producer, situates her authority over an experience she dispenses in short selections, as if inhibitions were momentarily thrust aside.

This fictionalization of the author—reproducing her as authority over her work—also sediments anecdote as non-fiction. Veracity is its intrigue, supported by the latent suggestion that it emerges reluctantly, as a matter of some delicacy.

The anecdote is the story you'd rather not tell Mom. If it can humiliate its protagonist, it must be true.

And yet, this power must also be open to abuse, and here Delany's anecdotal digressions—which may, in fact, be anything but digressions—call attention to themselves as fictions. Surely they hold truth—but surely anything that seems *so* conveniently matched to the purposes of its author's essays must be read with suspicion. Suspended between the real some would call experience and the apparatus of the story as vehicle for fiction, the anecdote again evades judgment, refuses to appease any members of the audience who wish to separate (however fictional the separation may be) the real from the unreal.

Observation: once again, essaying to pin down one point or another, I try to capture an essence and come up empty-handed. Hunting for a thesis on anecdote, the essay goes home hungry. Then again, isn't it just like an essay to fantasize something so ethereal, so mysterious, so resistant to capture?

Academics fall in love with what they can't understand. On the verge of epiphany, the essay climaxes: its peak can only be reached by veering away from its desired completion.

Postmodernists revel in what slips between gaps, can't be caught on tape, escapes conventional terms, collapses binaries, combines genres, eclipses logic. Don't let this thing be the anecdote. No more clichés about evasive strategies; the anecdote may be democratic after all, what otherwise should be called tyrannical. Slipped into discourse, its seductive qualities entrap and control.

After all, the anecdote has a function elsewhere; its home isn't the essay, but the wedding or funeral. In the loosely religious, somewhat Jewish, sometimes Christian, occasionally atheist middle-class American milieus with which I am most familiar, the anecdote emerges as the speaker's central recourse, her strategy for identifying brides and grooms or for eulogizing the deceased. In these settings, the anecdote condenses an individual into the symbolism of a single incident.

Another hypothesis: A story begins in movement, a re-entry into a system or series of circulations. It constructs a trajectory of fantasies and realities, a rippling of knowledge as from an already indiscernible locus, scattering of birds, wingbeats, airdrafts. Yet the story comes already wrapped in another discourse, disguised by critically engaged theories, postulates, positions and arguments.

"Etymologically, the term 'discourse,'" Delany tells us, "is a Latin word that refers to an old, oval, Roman race track... The spectators entered the central section of the track before the race, took their seats—or more often simply walked about from one side to the other—while the racers coursed around and around them... To explore a discourse... is inevitably to tell a story."[68]

Thus Delany's essay, "On the Unspeakable." Printed in columns that circle back on themselves, inviting the reader to leap in midstream and read until he returns to where he began, or to scan back and forth between the two columns until their simultaneous narratives converge, the essay proceeds without beginning or ending, revolving around the instabilities governing what can and cannot be spoken in any given setting. Delany's concern is, as he says, "the endlessly specialized tropes [...] required to speak or write about various topics at various anomalous places in our complex social geography."[69]

At the same time, characters inhabit this essay, appearing in brief but unforgettable anecdotes: Rose, the crack addict and prostitute, the ex-pimp named Red who obliges her by scratching her back, the young working class kid who masturbates and consumes his own semen. Their presence produces a profound disturbance, and through this disturbance, offers a marvelous and fascinating window into the many ways that discourse is normalized, contained, and, in many cases, self-censored.

What others call saliva is nothing other than the anecdote, that which lubricates discourse's foreskin; the professional academic who Delany's essays conjure must lick his lips and press them against the essay to peel back the foreskin of discourse.

Hypothesis: Mixing metaphors is the best way to assess the critical possibilities opened by the theatrical anecdotes that infuse Samuel R. Delany's critical essays.

Jack Spicer has written, "A metaphor is something unexplained—like a place in a map that says that after this is desert.

A shorthand to admit the unknown."[70] In my personal short-hand, an instant of self-pleasure is the easiest metonymy for the critical conclusion to which my essay never comes.

Observation: Every story unfolds amidst the theoretical chaffs of the culture that surrounds it. This fact, too, skirts Delany's theoretical engagements, in which the anecdote is never only digression, but serves as critical evidence that sexuality and sto-rytelling can't be disentangled. The striptease Roland Barthes has described as narrative reappears in Delany's theaters, in which "the *hope* of seeing the sexual organ," as Barthes puts it, is superseded by the possibility for sex to engender other engage-ments: interracial and cross-class discourse, an investigation of desire's endless reaches.[71] The anecdotes that chronicle these critical encounters, swaddled in discourse, move toward the unspoken horizon of desire.

My interest is in knowledge as bowline, the nonbinding knot Delany's anecdotes tie in discourse, through which memories and identities slip.

Perhaps the anecdote projects the figure of the author onto the wrinkles and folds covering what I have called the foreskin of discourse. Perhaps what my essay can't get back must be mea-sured in the hours I've spent masturbating under the guise of what must get done in order to begin my project.

Then again, in my ongoing fear that I am insufficiently prepared for the critical engagements I can't manage to make, I leave out footnotes and citations that ought to, were I more perspicacious, attest to my comfort as scholar; even as I try to be an academic, I find it necessary to discredit myself, to acknowledge my inability to properly situate my work within academia. In truth, I can only write as would-be, my essay is as yet only would-be, a series of propositions that can't go beyond the sense that Delany has managed, through his careful and consistent deployment of anecdote amidst criticism, to write my own hypotheses out from under me, even as he rewrites the relationship between the social self and the figure of the author.

Hypothesis: The risk and success of Delany's critical endeavors involves his careful self-referentiality; as risk, Delany's professional and professorial status hinges upon the reader's acceptance of his explorations of sexuality's permissible fringes; as success, his essays posit the potential for a reconstruction of the author as figure, an assertion of identity that returns the tweeded professorial figure to his secret weekend haunts and naked after work "hobbies" supposedly inadmissible as subjects of scholarly repute. If I could I would give my essay over to science, I'd bandage my prose to antibiotics and mail it in.

My knowledge of scientific method is perhaps the only scant area of knowledge lesser developed than my inability, already mentioned, to manage literature as a properly academic topic. If Delany has rewritten the figure of the author, I would like at once to investigate this rewriting, and at the same time disfigure myself as author, discredit myself as part of the process in the investigation I am proposing.

I'd like to speak of the anecdote, first-person tale of things unpublished.

I'd like to reawaken my narcolepsy, my boredom and my inability to read anything without a stimulant of some kind, preferably not available in your neighborhood drugstore.

I'd like to stop talking about masturbation.

I'd like to think that there could be a black market, profiteering in essays, in anecdotes. The professor was caught dealing in anecdotes. He fed his anemones on anecdotes. His prize angelfish swam on after death, the disembodiment of his empty discourse, the embodiment of its own anecdote, amphetamined through time...

"Objects, words must be led across time not preserved against it," writes Jack Spicer. He continues: "I yell 'Shit' down a cliff at an ocean. Even in my lifetime the immediacy of that word will fade. It will be dead as 'Alas.' But if I put the real cliff and the real ocean into the poem, the word 'Shit' will ride along with them, travel the time-machine until cliffs and oceans disappear."[72] The movie house encounters Delany chronicles open toward the ocean to which Spicer shouts "Shit," the ocean into which desire swims beyond the cliffs scaled by discourse. The anecdote is the shit that rides "until cliffs and oceans disappear."

Lament in Place of Hypothesis: If only writing an essay could recreate the glory holes in video arcades and porn shops now lining the streets to the north and south of the 42nd Street theaters Delany's essays recall: stick your dick through the hole; wait for lips to grip its rim and tongue and suck until release. That's what an essay should be like. Stick your language through the slot, let it drop, spill your letters.

Confession in Place of Observation: I mean to speak of the theater of desire, in which the theater is desire and desire is on display in the theater, unless this theater is also writing, and then there is the theater itself, the theater that appears in the essay by Samuel R. Delany, and I become confused as to whether the theater is a theater of desire, or the essay in which the theater appears is a theater of desire, or both the essay and the theater in the essay are theaters of desire. But it makes a nice title.

You can walk around with an idea and people usually aren't bothered by it. You can give it a name, call it a theater or desire. You can go and sit in a theater with your idea, but if it's the wrong theater and you act on your idea, and your idea rocks the bend in the normative mirror, you're in hot water. If you mix your metaphors in the wrong crowd you'll get caught with your shoe in your hand and the apple tree at your feet.

Let's reconsider an engagement with the impure discourses that inform Samuel Delany's essays: heartbeats or excretions or fists full of pages torn from Hart Crane, twisted and knotted into hempen cords wound round our wrists and ankles; we might free ourselves, formerly gagged and bound, from the summer camp called grammar, we might dream again climactic plea-sures under cover of some theater's recesses, our thoughts might effloresce like cauliflowered blisters covering chapped hands. Can we squeeze anecdotes out of discourse, can we offer them like astrolabes as gifts to itinerant readers?

If professor grows out of the verb *to profess*, to proclaim publicly, imagine the professor who turns up storyteller, neither the story-teller Benjamin tells us "returns from afar," nor the one who, he says, "has stayed at home," not the "resident tiller of the soil," but the storyteller who returns from the *demimonde*, the underworld, the theater in which the projector illuminating pornographic films casts covert sexual acts in shadow, discretion and ecstasy— the professor and professional storyteller thus returning, will he bring with him a new figure of the author, will he erect as sign of his profession transgression, he who writes into being his own undressing, his self-exposure writ large, whose discourse hitches instruments of analysis to mechanisms of desire, whose spittle wets renegade methods in order to slip sexual exploits like candlewicks into the flammable stacks of academic books...[73]

Let this storyteller be the storyteller I read in Delany's essays, the one to gather Spicer's "garbage of the real," that which "still reaches out into the current world making *its* objects, in turn, visible—lemon calls to lemon, newspaper to newspaper, boy to boy."[74]

NOTES

40. Samuel R. Delany, *The Fall of the Towers* (New York: Vintage Reprint, 2004; 1971); "The Tale of Plagues and Carnivals" appears as part of *Flight from Nevèrÿon* (Hanover, NH: Wesleyan UP, 1985), though its setting is New York City at the onset of the AIDS crisis, rather than the ancient land of Nevèrÿon. Throughout the *Nevèrÿon* series, K. Leslie Steiner and S.L. Kermit (ostensibly inventions of the author himself), contribute critical commentaries about the narrative's origins, possible forerunners or sources, and so on.

41. Samuel R. Delany, *Shorter Views: Queer Thoughts & The Politics of the Paraliterary* (Hanover, NH: Wesleyan UP, 1999), 53.

42. Samuel R. Delany, *Longer Views: Extended Essays* (Hanover, NH: Wesleyan UP, 1996), 120.

43. *Shorter Views*, 11.

44. Michel Foucault, *The Archaeology of Knowledge and The Discourse on Language,* trans. A.M. Sheridan Smith (New York: Pantheon Books, 1972), 216.

45. *Shorter Views*, 48.

46. Muriel Rukeyser, *The Life of Poetry* (Ashfield, MA: Paris Press, 1996), 162.

47. Samuel R. Delany, *Dahlgren* (New York: Bantam Books, 1975).

48. Kathleen Stewart, *A Space on the Side of the Road: Cultural Poetics in an Other America* (Princeton UP, 1996), 71.

49. *Shorter Views*, 54.

50. Walter Benjamin, *Illuminations,* trans. Harry Zohn. (New York: Schocken Books, 1968), 87.

51. Samuel R. Delany, *Times Square Red, Times Square Blue* (New York: NYU Press, 1999), 111.

52. This entire paragraph might be superfluous; then again, by encouraging compliance and conformity to the standards of academic discourse, even the most well-meaning left-leaning scholars might be enforcing fundamentally reactionary principles and policies.

53. *Times Square Red, Times Square Blue,* 22.

54. Ibid., 23.

55. Frank O'Hara, *The Collected Poems of Frank O'Hara,* ed. Donald Allen (Berkeley: U. of California Press, 1995), 260.

56. Ibid., 371-372.

57. Joe LeSueur and Bill Berkson, *Digressions on Some Poems by Frank O'Hara: A Memoir* (New York: Farrar, Straus and Giroux, 2003), 201.

58. *Shorter Views,* 60.

59. *Digressions on Some Poems by Frank O'Hara,* 39.

60. Ibid., 40.

61. *Shorter Views,* 46.

62. *Longer Views,* 138.

63. Jane Gallop, *Anecdotal Theory* (Durham: Duke UP, 2002), 82.

64. *Shorter Views,* 62-63.

65. Maurice Blanchot, *The Blanchot Reader,* ed. Michael Holland (Oxford: Blackwell, 1996), 273.

66. *Anecdotal Theory,* 86.

67. Ibid., 163.

68. *Shorter Views,* 13-14.

69. Ibid., 62.

70. Jack Spicer, *The Collected Books of Jack Spicer*, ed. Robin Blaser (Santa Rosa: Black Sparrow Press, 1999), 162.

71. Roland Barthes, *The Pleasure of the Text*, trans. Richard Howard (New York: Hill and Wang, 1975), 17.

72. *Collected Books*, 25.

73. *Illuminations*, 84-85.

74. *Collected Books*, 34.

3

ROBERT GRENIER'S ENDANGERED WORKS

"Robert Grenier's most recent writing," Stephen Ratcliffe suggests, "may well be the last word on what's new in American poetry today." Seven years ago, I started working on a short essay about Robert Grenier's "most recent writing": the series of drawing poems he began in the mid-1980s, and which he is still working on today. "I'm reading a poem," I wrote in my essay—which is no more true today, than it was seven years ago, when I first wrote it. The poem I wanted to pretend I was "reading" was one that I had copied from an enlarged color print, set into a simple black frame, and hanging on the wall of Grenier's bedroom—in other words, a digital reproduction of the original, hand-drawn poem.

My own interest in Grenier's writing had led me to the only place where I knew I could find the bulk of this work; at the time, that place was the half-a-house in Bolinas, California, that Bob had been renting for a few decades.[75] The problem readers face is twofold; though the poems may be "what's new," as Stephen Ratcliffe says, they "may also be all but impossible to read, since Grenier's latest works are written by hand—his hand's own illegible (but often exactly 'drawn') 'scrawl'—in four colors, Faber-Castell 'uni-ball' black, blue, green and red—therefore impossibly expensive to print, therefore all but unavailable to anyone who would read them."[76]

The vast majority of Grenier's drawing poems—more than 170 notebooks, each containing 212 pages, and thus as many as 36,000 hand-drawn poems—remain unpublished. And while libraries at Stanford and Yale house notebooks 1 thru 10 and 11 thru 20, respectively, the rest of the notebooks have no guarantee of a future home.

When I first began this essay, I wanted to reproduce my reading of just one of these "all but impossible to read" poems. I wanted to write *as if* I were reading the poem, and although I couldn't even see the poem I was writing about, I wanted to convey the peculiar and distinct sensations that struck me upon first reading it. In its "rough translation," as Grenier calls such renderings, the poem I wanted to read might be written as follows: "MOON / IT'S / THE / RE."

"Speech," as Robert Creeley says, "is a mouth"—and so our voices echo in the orifice otherwise known as language, "MOON" of the repeating "O." "How gradually the moon climbs," I write, thinking of the letters that make up Bob's "MOON." So too might the poem reveal by degrees. Bob mentions a poem by Matthew Arnold: "With tremulous cadence slow," Arnold writes in "Dover Beach." A slow-moon crawl, as roundabout as can be—as if to mirror the moon's own reflective nature, the poem unfolds at that deliberate pace with which the moon rises—until at last, "IT'S / THE / RE."

If you could go and read this poem as it is drawn, in Bob's hand, how long would it take you to make out the individual characters? You might not recognize any letter, not immediately—and so you might not read it at all, at least, not according to any conventional sense of what "reading" usually entails. Nonetheless, you might begin to understand the value in using different colors of ink: when lines break, colors change; the letters that make up a word—or part of a word, in one line—can be distinguished from other letters, drawn in other colors, on other lines. Your task might begin to feel almost archaeological. To discover any single letter presents its own difficulties, and whatever lines, curves, and strokes make up one letter, might interrupt, or appear to have been interrupted, by the lines, curves, and strokes making up the others—or they share lines and curves, here and there, and borrow from one another, or disappear into one another, cross over, come back to themselves, go missing.

This essay might be a repeated attempt to reread "MOON / IT'S / THE / RE," to linger under the sign of its echo, "MOON" of the repeating "O." In the broken English of the fortune cookie one finds this same "O," "never odd or even," unintelligible and profound, as open as it is closed. The moon is not only the moon, but what it reflects—that is to say, the sun. Or, as the ancient Egyptians would have it, *Re*, more commonly translated *Ra*. God of the sun, origin of everything.

"For me," Bob writes, " 'RE' is also 'again'—so 'MOON' is 'there again' (to direct perception)—*seen* to be partially obscured by 'clouds' (layers of drawn lines / marks), then reappearing (gone)… 'the/re again'… etc." And one could—or rather, "you could," Bob says, "relate this experience" (of trying to make out the letters in the poem) to that of "trying to *see the moon* amidst changing, complicated, moon-lit clouds." And in so doing, "bring your analysis of 'problems' involved in trying to read the poem back to the 'statement' the poem is concerned to make…"

Yesterday—or, to be more accurate, on what was *actually* yesterday, a few years ago—and what I should continue to call "yesterday," so as to fortify the fictional chronology that helps to structure this essay—I recorded a public conversation with Robert Grenier.

Today I'm sitting "here." In an apartment, in Brooklyn. Trying to finish an essay that I started seven years ago. About Robert Grenier's drawing poems.

Sometimes it takes a long time not to say too much about anything. It's hard, too—maybe that's why it takes a long time.

On the other hand, it's easy to say lots about nothing—lots about nothing can be said "pretty quick," as they say—which is why you might think there would be a lot more time left over for not saying too much about anything, but that ain't the case.

If an essay can be considered more or less fictional, certainly this is one.[77] Certainly, one says in the essay. This essay is critically deficient. Short on fundamentals, loose with facts. If it's not plainly fiction, one might ask about the ethics of pretense, the morality of the rhetorical sleight-of-hand. "I'm reading a poem..."

Let's pretend I'm going to stop talking about myself for a minute.

I'll speak for you instead. "You" "read" by feeling your way, trying gradually at first, very slowly, and then gradually also finding something, a familiar shape perhaps, trying to see more of—to follow—not knowing what to follow next, actually—but somehow still managing to follow a single line of blue *here*, to where it curves or changes course *there*, intersects another line (red *here*, or green, *there*), searching for another, so as to assemble, one character at a time, something out of that written language that you know and yet do not know… but it continues, this moving of the eyes, back and forth, searching for one familiar curve here, another familiar line there… one might measure the time it takes, perhaps one might even read aloud, even to oneself, as if to prove that those hand-made shapes transcend the ink and paper from which they are made and vanish as sounds in the ether.

Still, reading is a problem, a great problem. So dumb, and so simple—almost impossible, because it *is* when you *are*, and then it seems it *isn't* when you *aren't*, and because it happens in time, and then you are always running out of time, and still you never know how it *is*, and at the same time, how it *isn't*.

What you haven't read might not exist, so long as you don't read it—but it's there, all the same, if—or, when—you do.

This could be an essay about preservation, or conservation. Every essay could be that, perhaps every essay *must* be that—just as every essay, especially this one, posits an imaginary future, in which someone reads something.

In the poem you are reading—that you are reading "right now," "as we speak"—"MOON / IT'S / THE / RE"—the conjunction "IT'S" is such a difficult thing to read. It could be that the "S" puts you on skates, invites you to step onto what looks like pretty thin ice—and how strong can "is" be, shortened to "it's," tethered to "t" and deprived of its rightful "i"—all this, after having served for so long as that giving and passive, frozen thing, that "is"—what *is* it, this "is," and how long before it cracks, and how do you keep your breath when it does? Does the 'S' seem to summon, for you (as Bob notes that it does, for me), "frost on the windowpane?" Or is it your own breath that fogs the glass?

Wipe it clean if you'd like, the moon offers no counsel. "I get a sense that one *sees* (recognizes) 'MOON' as a 'cold' (alien), 'neutral' (other) thing, not 'he' or 'she,' an 'it'—out there, in space... an icy (lifeless?) presence," Bob writes.

"MOON / IT'S / THE / RE." Well, of course it is. Then again, there's more than one person who's noticed—even you, I would think, you yourself *must* have noticed—and there's many more that's done and seen and know'd at least as much as you might think you yourself to know, some who's come before you, and some who's bound to follow after, and who'd readily agree, if given the chance, and they just might be, who knows, the point is, you and them's likely to agree—that knowing what is, and what ain't, ain't always so easy.

What it means "to be" ("or, not...") is, of course, *the stuff of literature*, or so they say. And if you can't make out what it is about "IT'S" that makes it what it is, well, there's obviously some precedence here. What it means that there is an "it," or an "is," *is* hard to understand, should be hard. As hard as language is difficult—as difficult as being is hard—and no less precarious. There could be a value in that which is difficult and precarious, though ours is not, so far as most things go, a culture that readily appreciates difficult and precarious things—and even language is spilled and spouted and spewed, as if drawn from some infinitely deep wellspring.

Talk has never been so cheap, I guess—but I'm thinking of Bob's drawing poems, how they contrast with the endless blather of this bloated culture. Poets have long considered theirs an endangered art. I have begun to wonder whether its survival might not actually depend upon such works as Bob's drawing poems, and others like them, in which whatever language is, or whatever it is that language does, is whittled down to its most basic, fundamental units. In this case, the hand-drawn letter. In order to best preserve that species of language from which poetry springs, more time and space should be given to the distinguishing marks, scratches, and scribbles—the curious "scrawl"—in which these hard-to-read poems have been written.

To shape the line and make a letter, to learn the discipline in one's own hand, even before one has learned to read—handwriting could be the first experience of writing-as-possession, not to mention reading as such: "it's me," "here I am." "This letter is *mine*, I *made* it"; "I am that letter, it *made* me"; "This is how *I* make an 'I,'" "This is how an 'I' makes 'me.'"

Bob has shown me what might be described as a self-portrait, appearing in one or another of his notebooks: an outline of one hand, as drawn by the other. No words in that poem, or rather, no letters, but still, the poem is there, inscribed by his own hand, as they say.

Hand of the poet, body of language, shadow of the maker under the "MOON" of the repeating "O."

When translated as fable, a protagonist inhabits this essay—a traveler, or so it is written, who sets out to find the moon of the repeating "O." In another version of this essay, the author announces his practice as interruption, claims to make of interruption a "critical methodology," a way of being.

To be is hard, there is precedence—and there is precedence for the hand-made poem, and for handwritten notebooks that cannot be published—at least, not so as to capture what they are. Consider, for example, the work of Emily Dickinson, as described in Susan Howe's *My Emily Dickinson*.

The essay could be hypothetical, a series of propositions made across time, so as to inch closer to death. I was going to say, "so as to inch closer to truth," but death has certainty on its side. And if correspondence to reality is the measure of truth, death is not only more certain than truth, but also more truthful—it could be that, "truth be told," the essay is on loan from death—which may or may not provide evidence for the ostensible usefulness of the hypothesis, i.e., "[the essay] could be hypothetical, a series of propositions," "so as to inch closer to death."

"Truth and death belong to the same country club."

Philip Marlowe might have said that, but he would have had in mind an actual place, like a real country club somewhere. With a golf course and swimming pool, a banquet hall, tennis courts—clay courts, the color of ruby-red grapefruits, just before they go rotten and grow mold. The whole enterprise, cut out of some corner of the orange groves to the north, or the east. In that *who cares* region, forty minutes from Pasadena, an hour and a half in rush hour traffic.

You can think all you want about traffic, as for me, I'm thinking of the drawing poems, which is not the same as reading them. You can think yourself silly, and you still can't get your hands on the notebooks. The problem is, how to put them somewhere so someone can read them, before something happens to them, before they get split up and sold to various collectors, or vanish into that sinkhole of collectibles and relics, art objects and curiosities...

The impenetrable rush rush rush of what they call life—the question is, could there be poetry that might could muster enough courage to resist? Can a slow, obscure, possibly fruit-less effort to capture or frame or freeze some piece outside that rush—"memorialize" it, say—and what would it mean to "memorialize" "some piece" "outside that rush"? Or, can *one* such effort—which might not have been such an effort at all, but is now, in the absence of reading, being imagined as one, by the "author" of this "essay"—can one such effort simply *be* for any length of time, beyond its moment of composition, without being swallowed in the overflowing currents, without groveling for spare change from the Masters of Culture and Economics?

The late afternoon here in Brooklyn offers no answers; school's out, it's the red light hustle for you, and for everyone else. Stop at the greasy spoon and then home for television and microwaved popcorn, internet porn. Zeroes and ones: this is what they now call a "social network."

Consider the premise that each of us has, as days pass, flashes of recognition—moments when what surrounds us is seen for what it is, as what is—or, to vulgarize Heidegger, when "what is" shines forth into language—or plunges, as if dropped from some great height, deep into the river of perception, bobbing to the surface and diving under again, propelled against the rushing current of sensation, however briefly, by some unknown force—and then acquiescing at last to the icy waters, swiftly carried to sea, sinking somewhere in the Mariana Trench of the mind.

It's nothing really, a sprout or cloud that casts its shadow around—or, in the shadow of that shadow, some simple word: sprout, cloud, round—it may be what they call the "mind" engulfs the letters, or maybe the letters cling to that fast-sinking thing, glimpsed in the curvature of the vowels—in eddies where flows break on consonants, where language sprays and swirls—language become whitewater—whirlpools where diphthongs press upon the voice as vortex, orifice—layers of sediment through which words seep, dripping toward some wellspring, mouth open to light, light seeking sound out from the absence of being—being absent, but for that channel from which the voice issues...

It all might just as well sink, but if it's the something I'm think-ing of here, even as it sinks, it slides past a barnacled porthole in the leaky vessel of the mind, witness to language, or witnessed in language. Set or sent to another measure and time. Such a something seems to me *to be*—or, what *is*—in this poem, or that one—in Bob's drawing poems.

The relationship between this measure, and that one—or your moon, and this "MOON." "IT'S" is—and has—in Bob's poem—those three letters, except that they're not the same letters. How to explain this mysterious "is" and "isn't," this sameness and difference? The curious, familiar "I"—rigid, upright, upstand-ing—in short, a serious character, by most standards; a plinth or pedestal, commonly used to display cultural riches, as well as a utilitarian device, against which a body might lean; a structural component—a pole or post of some kind, a weight-bearing pillar perhaps—providing support for story upon story, monolithic edifice…

Rest in its shadow while you can. Beyond the border, across the "T," stretches that long road where "S" curves, leading to who knows where.

Philip Marlowe leans under the shadow of the "I" and offers you a cigarette. "If your luck's as lousy as mine," he says, "the 'S' leads to that *who cares* region, forty minutes from Pasadena, an hour and a half in rush hour traffic."

Nobody but Marlowe has Marlowe's luck; if your luck's like *mine*, you'll find that the poems are where you go to lose your discourse. To see what you can't say, what you don't have words for, what your "critical discourse" can't hack.

In trying to describe what these poems "do," I find that words fail me, I'm not sure what it is I want to say, I am simply and completely puzzled—and, pleased. First, by my inability—and then, by my ability—to do what, I wonder, and why? To become literate, and then to become illiterate, again? Or is it the other way around? To re-learn how to identify this letter, and that one? To remember how, and when, to put the letters together, or to keep them apart?

I wonder if I know what it means to be literate, if that's what I am—to come stumbling against a four-line poem made of just a few short words that I might have learned before I could walk, and to find myself reduced to the basic repeating of those words, out loud, or silently, to myself—inventing a sort of chronology that proceeds one letter at a time, stripped of the usual internal theoretical digressions or elaborations, having few (if any) immediate "literary" associations or philosophical reflections, becoming gradually aware of a silence, an absence of what I want to call analytical background noise—nothing in my mind whatsoever, except for what the poem says, and perhaps, as with "MOON," some sound-image of the word-thing—either as it exists in my memory of the "real thing," or as it appeared in some mediated image I have seen at one time or another, a painting or otherwise "manufactured" replica—a word-sound-thing-image-memory-feeling...

What else did you want, after all? And could it be that there has never really been anything more? Or rather, why did you ever want anything more than that, from a poem, or from whatever it is, that it is—there, or here?

I don't know. I encourage you to do the same. Lose your discourse, find a way.

To read, I mean. Robert Grenier's drawing poems.

NOTES

75. As I was working on this essay, Bob moved to Vermont.

76. "Grenier's Scrawl" appears in *Listening to Reading* (State University of New York Press, 2000).

77. "I haven't read enough criticism to know if this is an original thought," Bob writes. "Is it?" It is not original, nor is it widely accepted. Perhaps acknowledging expositional prose as a fundamentally creative endeavor, indistinguishable from fiction, would undermine the epistemological foundations of "the profession." At any rate, in the interests of full disclosure, the sentiments expressed by the sentence in question are not its only derivative elements; in addition, it seems likely that the structure of the sentence ("If [X] can be considered more or less [Y], certainly this is one") echoes one or more literary predecessors—Gertrude Stein, for example. "Some might opine," Bob notes, "that the act of 'reading' anything creates (and is, of useful necessity) a fictional encounter... since poem (or whatever) only lives in the time-it-takes (part of a lifetime) for a reader to imagine-into-existence what is being said (differently in each instance)..."

THE EXPERIMENTAL SUBJECT OF THE NARCO-IMAGINARY

1

Let me tell you how I'm feeling.

A wheelbarrow is a useful piece of equipment, you can roll it right into your most sensitive, most delicately tuned sentence, and there it sits, a perfectly handy impediment. So much depends upon the proper obstruction.

A proposal: the boundaries of the narco-imaginary depend upon the relationship between sensation and language. Sensation overlaps with feeling—that is to say, with emotion—and language flows like water through channels where feelings lie. Sometimes sharp and angled, cut from mountainous bedrock; elsewhere, filled with sediment, slow and curving, deliberate, alluvial: feelings give shape to language. At the same time, language works against feelings, courses through them, carving out emotional topographies.

For a long time now, I have wanted to write about feeling. Instead, when I try and write about feeling, I stall, drift, digress; I compile a roster of obstacles that prevent me from writing about feeling, I develop new and more intricate rationales to explain my failure.

I'm listening to music—the Grateful Dead. Judge me as you will. My topics scatter like powder over the surface of a mirror; as Harry Mathews says, in *20 Lines a Day*, "Whatever I write tells my story without my knowing it. What I'm aware of saying, even if it belongs to my story, is not the story I'm actually telling. What I'm actually telling is 'not that,' no, nor *that*. Whatever it is I'm telling will lie beyond (perhaps just beyond) what I say I'm saying, so that it doesn't matter much what I'm saying as long as I keep talking to myself (= writing)."

A short list of the luminaries who have served as experimental subjects of the narco-imaginary: the award-winning author, co-founder of The Paris Review, *and former CIA agent Peter Matthiessen, who was dosed with LSD, without warning, during the CIA's legendary informal investigations into acid as a tool for espionage; the experimental chemist and pharmacologist Gordon Alles, known as the first American to synthesize amphetamine, whose self-administered injections of speed helped to reveal its powerful psychoactive effects; Alexander Shulgin, the high priest of MDMA, who regularly sampled the 230-plus psychoactive compounds he discovered during his more than fifty-year career; Albert Hofmann, the Swiss chemist whose synthesis and fabled "accidental" ingestion of LSD-25 encouraged him to undertake further self-administered experiments with countless synthetic hallucinogens; not to mention the impressive roster of participants in Stanford University's experiments on LSD and other hallucinogens, including Allen Ginsberg; Jerry Garcia; Garcia's friend and songwriting collaborator, Robert Hunter; and Ken Kesey, whose experiences in the Stanford trials famously provided materials for his most well-known novel,* One Flew Over the Cuckoo's Nest.

2

In language, feelings lie.

I've been prescribed a drug that is likely, I am told, to influence my mood. Keep a journal, the doctor tells me, write about how you're feeling.

I accept his assignment: I myself become an experimental subject of the narco-imaginary.

The doctor asks me to make a daily entry, but I rarely do any writing at all, and most of the time, I can't write about how I'm feeling. When I do write about my feelings, I am an insincere journalist. I am more actively engaged in not-writing my journal; sometimes, instead of not-writing, I write something in my journal that sounds like what I think I'm supposed to feel, as a result of my medication. Occasionally, I almost feel like I *really* feel the way that I'm supposed to feel, and the way that I say that I'm feeling in my feelings journal. I have decided that any attempt to describe how one feels effects a change in how one is feeling, but I don't say so in my journal. Instead, I listen to music for hours; I fantasize about writing poems; I stare out the window; I read blog postings by others who have taken my medication; I read about its off-label uses, standard dosages, interactions with other prescriptions and over-the-counter drugs.

In his *Philosophical Investigations*, Wittgenstein is fascinated by the idea of expressing genuine feeling. "There is in general a complete agreement in the judgements of colours," Wittgenstein says. "This characterizes the concept of a judgement of colour." Feelings, Wittgenstein observes, are different: "There is in general no such agreement over the question of whether an expression of feeling is genuine or not," he writes. "What is most difficult here is to put this indefiniteness, correctly and unfalsified, into words."

Wittgenstein asks us to suppose that "every familiar word... carries an atmosphere with it in our minds, a 'corona' of lightly indicated uses." This corona, a flicker of thought sparked by some familiar word, might have the capacity to give to language what Wittgenstein calls the "if-feeling": unique sensations or emotions that do not adhere to the precise meaning of a word or phrase, but that can be sensed, nonetheless, so long as the word or phrase is heard in a specific context or atmosphere. To describe this "if-feeling"—the phenomenon by which words trigger sensations—Wittgenstein writes, "The if-feeling would have to be compared with the special 'feeling' which a musical phrase gives us."

How does music access feelings beyond language? "For me, music is ... it's emotional in nature," Jerry Garcia says. "It communicates emotionally. That's one of the things it does very well." Like any saint, martyr, or prophet, Jerry Garcia's story is a simple one: music comes pouring out a man who plays himself to death. Saint Jerry.

One day, I take a break from not-writing my feelings journal. I'm standing at the kitchen sink of my tiny Brooklyn apartment. I don't have air-conditioning, it's late July, 2014, and I'm sweating through my shirt, thinking about this essay, the book in which it might appear, the other essays that might be published alongside this one. Some of these essays were written before my oldest son was born; now he's eight, and my younger son is six. It's been four years since my divorce, and my kids have just left to spend two weeks in California with their mother, my ex-wife. I can't stomach the silence. I'm listening to Jerry Garcia's guitar, wandering up scales, and down—it's the Grateful Dead, "Eyes of the World," as taped in concert, circa 1973, and it's exquisite— and the more I listen, the more I cry, until I'm openly weeping over a stack of dirty dishes.

A wave of shame and embarrassment overtakes me: I have alienated my readers by confessing that I listen to the Grateful Dead, that I weep over the sound of Jerry Garcia's guitar. Bear with me. If you have never listened to the Dead, don't bother; if listening to "Eyes of the World" has never made you cry like it makes me cry, I can't explain why, there's no use trying; and if "Eyes of the World" makes you cry, I don't have to explain why. If you want to know how I feel, listen to the music that makes you cry.

3

The Grateful Dead emerged from Ken Kesey's acid tests, providing aural stimuli, or music, or both; at the acid tests, Neal Cassady (who also roomed with the band at their legendary San Francisco residence, 710 Ashbury Street) used their microphones for his spoken-word performances. Garcia's biographer, Blair Jackson, designates 1967 as the year that everything changed for the band. The Summer of Love turned the counterculture into a marketable commodity. Record companies descended upon San Francisco, signing bands that, like the Dead, had almost no reputation outside of the Bay Area. An early contract granted the band unlimited use of the recording studio, with the stipulation that the company would bill the band at an hourly rate for its usage; experimenting in the studio proved enormously engrossing—and resulted in an enormous debt. Coupled with legal fees stemming from drug busts in San Francisco and New Orleans, economic pressure forced the band to practice acoustically—it was cheaper—and resulted in what are widely regarded as the Grateful Dead's two best studio albums, both released in 1970: *Workingman's Dead* and *American Beauty*.

Still, what made the band distinct was the fact that, beginning in the early 1970s, it made a conscious effort to vary its set lists and repertoire from night to night; more importantly, the Dead initially turned a blind eye to concertgoers taping their live performances; in later years, they actively supported the practice, reserving a special audience section for tapers. Nick Paumgarten thus describes the culture of tape collecting and trading that emerged amongst the band's devotees: "If you took an interest, you'd copy a few tapes, listen to those over and over, until they began to make sense, and then copy some more. Before long, you might have a scattershot collection, with a couple of tapes from each year. It was all Grateful Dead, but because of the variability in sonic fidelity, and because the band had been at it for twenty years, there were many different flavors and moods. Even the compromised sound quality became a perverse part of the appeal. Each tape seemed to have its own particular note of decay, like the taste of the barnyard in a wine or a cheese."

In the annals of the narco-imaginary, the Grateful Dead might be classified as the discipline's longest-running unsanctioned experiment.

As Peter Gans has said of the band that Jerry Garcia made famous, and that made Jerry famous:

> Nobody wanted to pull the plug on [the Grateful Dead]—especially when it was raking in $50 million a year. The number of people on their payroll was one burden; the hundreds of other people whose income derived from the Grateful Dead was another planet's worth of weight; and then there was the happiness that the band brought to hundreds of thousands of people in the world.

I'd like to write about Jerry Garcia, and about the Grateful Dead, too. But mostly about Jerry Garcia. And about music and feeling, or perhaps feelings. About all four, or rather, all five: Jerry Garcia, the Grateful Dead, music, feeling—and feelings. Then again, in saying "feelings," I understand that there are more than five, with or without Jerry Garcia, and with or without the Grateful Dead.

I have forgotten to mention addiction, eager understudy to the indulgences proffered by the narco-imaginary.

The manifestation of addiction: those close to Jerry Garcia speculate that heroin narrowed his world. Behind the closed door of his dressing room, his habit kept him safe, remote, unavailable. My doctor speculates that my use of Adderall helped to drown out my habitual self-criticism. Static doubt: the constant background noise that I find myself battling, even now, as I imagine Jerry Garcia's need. To create a space, to be—not for others, not for anyone—space to be free from oneself, as much as from anyone else. At any moment, I might tune into the crackle and hiss of self-criticism that underscores everything I do. I'm no longer taking Adderall, and that makes it hard to write.

4

In *Philosophical Investigations*, Wittgenstein puzzles over the curious relationship between "internal speech," "saying inwardly"—and "saying," which is to say, the "outward" process of speaking: engaging the larynx, making sound. One can talk without thinking, but to do so is very different, Wittgenstein says, from thinking (silently). Moreover, it would be nonsensical to say that to engage in thought is to speak without speaking, or to speak to oneself; when a person says that he talks to himself—when he says, for example, "I tell myself," he is usually speaking to someone else. One thinks without thinking; to think, one does not need to say silently, to oneself, "Now I'm going to begin thinking," although one might quite consciously

- 168 -

choose to engage oneself in "internal speech." The phrase "saying inwardly" illuminates a confounding obscurity where language and thought diverge. "I can know what someone else is thinking," Wittgenstein writes, "not what I am thinking. It is correct to say 'I know what you are thinking,' and wrong to say, 'I know what I am thinking.' (A cloud of philosophy condensed into a drop of grammar.)"

"Tuned in on my own frequency / I watch myself looking," writes Philip Whalen. In the same poem—"Self-Portrait, From Another Direction"—Whalen writes, "I think, what is thinking / What is that use or motion of the mind that compares with / A wink, the motion of the belly."

"Tuned into one's own frequency," "watching oneself looking," "thinking, what is thinking," the narco-imaginary reflects upon itself, to itself. To make thinking of thinking a particular experience, a peculiar experience: to think of thinking, and while thinking of thinking, to seek the representation of this self-conscious consciousness, only to discover that consciousness, self and other, is "always already" transformed, transforming even as one attempts to perfect its representation.

At the same time, Whalen's poem suggests that, to understand the "motion of the mind," one's attention must travel. "What is that use or motion of the mind," he writes, "that compares with / A wink, the motion of the belly." Compare, refer, defer, deflect, redirect, go forth, go further; in order to think about thinking, let's remember this referential, deferential impulse; let's bow in respect to the poem as our wise and humble guide; let's imagine that deviations inspire discoveries; let's be mindful of the directive to express ourselves through an alternative organ, a wink of the eye, a motion of the belly, a different medium, another site on the body, a citation from the body of another text; let's forgive ourselves, in advance, if we refer endlessly to some elsewhere in the absence of any recognizable origin or essence.

A series of endlessly flowering arabesques, a set of Chinese boxes: the narco-imaginary traffics in repetition and cliché. In the drawer that holds the research I've done on my own *experimental subject*—the narco-imaginary—I have a file that is labeled, "the experimental subject of the narco-imaginary"; the experimental subject of the narco-imaginary *is* the experimental subject of the narco-imaginary.

The experimental subject of the narco-imaginary, European edition: Fritz Fränkel's notes on Walter Benjamin's hashish intoxication, or rausch (rush, high, delirium), 18 April 1931, as translated by Scott J. Thompson (Thompson's notes appear in brackets): "For long stretches of the rausch one can speak of a technical construction of a Rahmenerzählung *[link and frame story, story within a story]: two limbs of a mental image branch off from one another, raising the whole profusion of images in the space between to a new phase. One has to negotiate, so to speak, the 'open sesame' which is directed at the mental image. The mental image itself splits in two, opening the doorway to new treasure chests of images. This constantly repeated mechanism comprises one of the most amusing moments of the hashish rausch."*

Wink and one "I" closes. As the observer and the observed, the experimental subject of the narco-imaginary loses focus, swells, inflates: "A wink, the motion of the belly," Whalen writes; "motion," from Old French, "to move"; "belly," from

Old English, "to swell, to be inflated," "to blow into"; and so, to "watch [oneself] thinking" is to wink, to close the "I," to move, to swell, to inflate. The eye dilates and you glide, Lucy in the sky.

5

If we were to decide upon the narco-imaginary as a necessarily experimental subject, a subject that demanded from its scholars ever more expansive forms of study, analysis, and investigation, how might the body of the text serve such a subject, bear witness to its own transformation, give credence to the bewildering influence of the narco-imaginary? What is the shape of language under the influence of the narco-imaginary?

Walter Benjamin, 29 September 1928, Marseilles: "To get closer to the riddle of bliss in rausch one must reconsider Ariadne's thread. What delight in the mere act of unwinding a skein. And this delight is quite profoundly related to the delight of rausch, as it is to the delight in creative work. We go forward: but in doing so not only do we discover the bends of the cavern in which we venture forth, but rather we savor this happiness of discovery by virtue of that other rhythmical bliss which comes from unraveling a skein. Such a certainty from the intricately wound skein that we unravel—is that not the happiness of at least every prose form of productivity? And under hashish we are prose beings savoring at the peak of our powers."

Thinking of thinking, Terence McKenna quotes anthropologist Misia Landau: "'The twentieth-century linguistic revolution is the recognition that language is not merely a device for communicating ideas about the world, but rather a tool for bringing the world into existence." Thus, Landau writes, "Reality is not simply 'experienced' or 'reflected' in language, but instead is actually produced by language." "For the shaman," McKenna concludes, "the cosmos is a tale that becomes true as it is told and as it tells itself."

As Avital Ronell observes, to study a drug is to study an object that "resists the revelation of its truth to the point of retaining the status of absolute otherness." The problem is not so much how to understand "drugs," or how to define "addiction," but how to explore that which brings you to the very limits of your own language, the language of others: "The problem," Ronell concludes, "is signaled ... in the exhaustion of language."

Several years ago, I began taking Adderall—speed—to cope with ADHD. As soon as I took one pill, I became a witness to, and participant in, a debate over whether or not I should take another pill. As I found with cigarettes, the benefit of one cigarette—the one you're actually smoking, in a given instant— is the promise that you will have another one, later on. With amphetamines, the premise of productivity became a sort of counter-measure, or counter-narrative—a quest narrative, or an illness narrative, or both. How much had I done, or would I be capable of doing, on one pill? After taking one pill, it seemed likely that taking another would serve my purposes just as well—better, in fact—because the first pill really seemed to be doing very little, as evidenced by the fact that I was doing very little, really, except worrying over how much work I had not done, yet. Very well then, I would take another. In fact, I would take two, so as to notice something—so as to feel the push of the pill, that is to say, of the first pill, as well as the second and third—and thereby produce, by a sum far greater than its parts, a workload far surpassing what could be done after taking just one pill—as well as what could be done by taking each of the subsequent pills, that is to say, the second, and the third, one at a time, at the recommended intervals—which I might have done, of course, had I not already taken three.

A nervous handshake between body and mind seals the covenant they call addiction. The future is lit. As Jerry Garcia said of cocaine, "It's like a melody you can't get out of your head." In the words of Avital Ronell, drugs "are not so much about seeking an exterior, transcendental dimension—a fourth or fifth dimension—rather, they explore *fractal interiorities.*"

Walter Benjamin, under the influence of hashish, 15 January, 1928: "As for our own distracted, abrupt switch from the subject under discussion ... we are endlessly allured with whatever we are directly engaged in discussing; we fondly stretch out our arms towards whatever we have a vague notion of. Barely have we touched it, however, than it disappoints us corporeally: the object of our attention withers away under the touch of language."

6

These were the years—these have been the years—without dreams. I don't remember my dreams, if I have them—I don't know. I think my dreams have gone with feeling. If you're not feeling, you're not feeling bad. If you're not dreaming, you have no bad dreams. Facing the vacancy of my dreams, thinking of not feeling, I almost ache. I could say that I'm sad for not having dreams, for not feeling, but I would be approximating a feeling where there is no feeling. I could say I think I'm feeling something for the dreams I don't have, but I'm not sure. I think I'm placing a feeling next to the vacancy where dreams should be, perhaps because I think others might think or feel something in reaction to the blank I'm trying to describe.

I might be getting ahead of myself; I am talking about feeling when I had wanted to talk about something else, whereas I had thought that, by talking about something else, I would be able to talk about feeling.

I'm trying to name the feeling you think I might possess, or should possess, according to my vacancies, lacks, blanks. Blank sleep, emotional vacancy.

Townes Van Zandt sits in the kitchen of a ramshackle house with a broken-down guitar. A woman does the dishes.[78] Seymour, an elderly man in a cowboy hat, enters and sits behind Van Zandt's right shoulder. There are people you can't see, but you can hear them in the background, singing along to the Guy Clark song, "That Old Time Feeling." Seymour is black; everyone else in the clip is white. The woman stops washing dishes to come and sit next to Seymour. Van Zandt tells a story; the film jumps ahead. The story Van Zandt tells has been truncated by the editing, but it seems to be about Van Zandt carrying Seymour back home when Seymour has had to much to drink. Laugher fills the room. The film jumps again, and Seymour speaks: "But now then on the other hand according to Mr. Van Zandt's statement, he has also seen me sit down where there's a lot of whiskey, like we've got whiskey here now, but he didn't see me drink all of it. I would drink some and walk away from it. And he's also felt kind of embarrassed because he's offered me whiskey, and I didn't want it. And he'd ask me, was I angry with him. I wasn't angry, I just didn't want no more whiskey." Van Zandt nods, the film jumps again. "This is the first song I ever wrote," says Van Zandt.

> Sometimes I don't know where this dirty road is taking me
> Sometimes I can't even see the reason why
> I guess I keep on gamblin', lots of booze and lots of ramblin'
> It's easier than just a waitin' around to die

I'd like to say something about this scene, about the ways it condenses or encapsulates themes—music, addiction, feeling—crucial to my purpose. These are men who feel, these are men feeling. Men drinking and feeling, or men drinking feeling. Does it matter they are men? She does the dishes. Perhaps it's an allegory: the patriarchal misery of Southern manhood.

What I'd like to say lies in that sink someplace where an unidentified woman washes dishes. I want to write about feeling, but I'm already trapped in a room full of men, singing and drinking. I would like to talk about feeling, but it's been rinsed clean.

I'm watching an interview with Townes Van Zandt, a "cult figure," as they say. Other terms associated with Van Zandt: "drunkard," "junkie," "outlaw country," "legendary," and "shock therapy" (to which Van Zandt was subjected after a brief and unsuccessful stint as a student at the University of Colorado). In the interview, he's sitting in front of what looks like a small house, palm trees in the background. There's a young woman who asks him about his best-known song, "Pancho and Lefty." "What's that song about?" she says.

This question is a bad question, I think—I am sorry for her. And I am ashamed, perhaps I am being unfair to her, perhaps my criticism of her question exposes my own biases. In truth, I don't know anything about music, she might know a lot more than I will ever know about music, for all I know she's a musician, a famous one, perhaps. Still, I am sorry for her, I wish that someone had told her that this question is a bad question— and I am sorry for him, because he is dead, and because he is considered underappreciated, and because I want more for him perhaps, I want him to be given something he never was, and never will be.

Maybe I am wrong in wishing something different for Townes Van Zandt; maybe there are those who knew him who would say that he was not a nice person, or that he deserved to live in squalor, that it was his own choice, just as he chose heroin and alcohol. "When someone's as good as Townes was, and more people still don't know about it, it's Townes's own fault," says Steve Earle. Steve Earle launched his career as a singer and songwriter by seeking out, and ultimately joining, the circle of musicians orbiting this man, his idol, Townes Van Zandt. Still, I am sorry for Townes Van Zandt when I hear the interviewer ask him, "What's that song about?" I imagine that it's not without effort that he maintains a straight face. He answers without condescension.

Of course, he doesn't answer, not straightaway, as they say. He appears to detour, he tells a story about getting stopped by cops in the middle of the night somewhere in Texas. He gets out of the vehicle and walks back to talk to the cops. They say he was speeding. He's apologetic, tries to be polite; he says he's a songwriter, and he's got the band in the car, and they're late for a gig. "No shit," one cop says; the other cop says, "How about telling us one of the songs you've written?" "Well, alright, sure," Van Zandt obliges: "'Pancho and Lefty.'" "*You* wrote 'Pancho and Lefty?'" "No shit, officer." "Pancho and Lefty?" "No shit, officers." General hilarity in the squad car, to wit: the officers—one Latino, and one Caucasian—are known in their department as "Pancho and Lefty." Van Zandt shrugs. "I guess it's a song about them."

7

The experimental subject straddles the threshold between empirical scientific discourse and literary discourse. As "evidence" for the ways in which drug use alters or supplements the subject's experience, the text produced by the experimental subject is fraudulent, duplicitous, corrupt: there is no means with which language can fully articulate unique individual experience through the trope of the experimental subject.

In her attempt to write about literature and addiction—to conduct what she calls a "narcoanalysis"—Avital Ronell confronts "an object that splits existence into incommensurable articulations." Drug use, Ronell observes, is antagonistic to literary ambition: "Considered non-productive and somehow irresponsible, a compulsive player of destruction, Being-on-drugs resists the production of meaning."

To raise the blinds, so as to witness another manifestation of the experimental subject of the narco-imaginary, we might call upon Albert Hoffmann's legendary (if accidental) experiment, circa 1943. Dr. Hoffmann notices that he does not feel well, and decides that he must leave work early: "At home I lay down and sank into a not unpleasant intoxicated-like condition, characterized by an extremely stimulated imagination. In a dreamlike state, with eyes closed (I found the daylight to be unpleasantly glaring), I perceived an uninterrupted stream of fantastic pictures, extraordinary shapes with intense, kaleidoscopic play of colors. After some two hours this condition faded away."

In the days that follow, Dr. Hoffmann concludes that his unanticipated experience must have resulted from his coming into contact with the substance he crystallized that same afternoon, a synthetic variant of the naturally-occurring fungus known as ergot. Of course, Dr. Hoffmann has discovered lysergic acid diethylamide—according to the research protocols of the lab, the precise name for this compound is "LSD-25."

Three days later, Dr. Hoffmann consumes .25 mg of LSD-25. Having planned his self-administered dosage as an experiment, he hopes to keep careful notes. On April 19th, he writes, "Taken diluted with about 10 cc water. Tasteless. 17:00: Beginning dizziness, feeling of anxiety, visual distortions, symptoms of paralysis, desire to laugh.... Home by bicycle. From 18:00... most severe crisis."

Dr. Hoffmann subsequently explains that the writing of these last three words, "most severe crisis," require incredible effort. He summons his friend, a doctor, to come and examine him; his vital signs are fine, the doctor says; except for whatever Dr. Hoffmann imagines to be wrong with him, nothing whatsoever *appears* to be wrong with him.

Thereafter, Dr. Hoffmann's trip continues rather pleasantly: "I could begin to enjoy the unprecedented colors and plays of shapes that persisted behind my closed eyes," he recalls. "Kaleidescope, fantastic images surged in on me, alternating, variegated, opening and then closing themselves in circles and spirals, exploding in colored fountains, rearranging and hybridizing themselves in a constant flux."

"Unprecedented," indeed. And yet, the description Dr. Hoffman provides seems hardly unprecedented, for it resembles a host of preceding descriptions, written by other experimental subjects. The only difference is that, rather than ingesting LSD-25, Hoffman's predecessors have ingested the hallucinogenic compound found in the mescal buttons of the peyote cactus, otherwise known as mescaline.

The experimental subject of the narco-imaginary is a counter-cultural idol, an icon, and a literary figure; even in the ostensibly objective "scientific" documents from clinical trials, the experimental subject remains a fabrication, a fictive character through which the effects of a given substance are measured, demonstrated, imagined.

Consider Silas Weir Mitchell, precursor to Freud, notorious as a pioneering practitioner of the resting cure (prescribed for those patients, mostly—though not all—women, suffering from nervous disorders of the day, such as neurasthenia or hysteria); Mitchell's patients included the legendary feminist intellectual and writer, Charlotte Perkins Gilman. Gilman underwent the resting cure under Dr. Mitchell's care, an experience that she fictionalized in her most well-known story, "The Yellow Wall-Paper."

In Gilman's story, the narrator has been confined in the attic of a rented country house for the summer as part of the resting cure prescribed by her husband, John, who is also a physician. As Gilman's tale unfolds, the narrator begins to hallucinate, watching as a woman just like herself seems to materialize out of the shadows and patterns on the wallpaper of her room. A phantom woman thus stares back, observing the observer, who is both comforted and tormented by these visions: "The outside pattern is a florid arabesque, reminding one of a fungus... imagine a toadstool in joints, an interminable string of toadstools, budding and sprouting in endless convolutions."

Published in 1892, Gilman's text might be considered the abstinent godmother to an "interminable string" of texts, "budding and sprouting in endless convolutions," documenting personal experiments with peyote, LSD, and psilocybin. Four years after the appearance of "The Yellow Wall-Paper," Silas Weir Mitchell published the first widely-read account of peyote intoxication, "The Effects of Anhelonium Lewinii (The Mescal Button)." Having been given the drug and told of its properties by a fellow physician, one D.W. Prentiss—a physician who not only tested peyote on himself and wrote about his self-experimentation, but who also offered peyote to the medical students he taught in Washington, D.C.—Mitchell explains that he "made a trial of the drug by taking it."

Despite his best attempts to record his experiences, Silas Weir Mitchell confesses that he is incapable of documenting "this land of fairy colours," the visions that arise as the peyote takes hold. "Were I to take mescal again," he writes, "I should dictate to a stenographer all that I saw and in due order. No one can hope to remember for later record so wild a sequence of colour and of forms."

In order to make up for what has been left out of his own record, Mitchell attaches an appendage, an account sent him by his friend and fellow physician, one Dr. Eshner. "When my eyes closed I became conscious of a series of visual impressions, in most of which colour sensations were present," writes Eshner. "The pictures were characteristically kaleidoscopic, particularly as regards uniformity of arrangement.... The designs were various; some were Oriental, with stars and crescents.... others were mosaic in arrangement; some were screen-like; some fern-like; some showed chased figures.... all sorts of new designs, fresco work, porcelain decorations, tapestry figures, intricate laces, parquetry, diagrams."

Witness, several years later, British physician Henry Havelock Ellis, who publishes an account that is, as he writes in a footnote, an account of an account: "I published a somewhat briefer account of this experiment in... *Contemporary Review*... This paper also contains the interesting results of an experiment on an artist friend; further remarks were published... in *Lancet* ..." In the same footnote, Ellis writes that his accounts, or his accounts of accounts, have spurred additional self-experiments by others: "These papers attracted the attention of Dr. Walter Dixon," Ellis writes, "who made many experiments on himself... published... in an interesting article."

While noting the contributions of Prentiss and Mitchell before him, not to mention his own contributions to his new contribution, Ellis again attempts to describe the "delicious effects" of his experience. And yet, Ellis ultimately confesses that, "the chief character of the visions is their indescribableness." Not to be deterred, Havelock Ellis continues: "sometimes, however, they are like clusters of jewels—some bright and sparkling, others with a dull rich brilliance. Again they resemble a vast collection of the glistering, iridescent, fibrous wings of gorgeous insects.... if I had to describe the visions in one word, I would say that they were living arabesques."

8

Of Walter Benjamin's writings collected in *On Hashish*, Marcus Boon writes, "part of the charm of the texts collected here stems from the profound confusion concerning subjectivity (not to mention objectivity) they display: as you read through these 'protocols' sometimes written by the user, sometimes by an observer, sometimes both, or through Benjamin's 'own' writings, in which he laces together a montage of quotes from other authors, it becomes increasingly difficult to remember who is writing and who is being written about." Benjamin, the original plagiarist; if Havelock Ellis could have anticipated Benjamin's techniques, he might have simply quoted Charlotte Perkins Gilman's anticipatory, yet ostensibly sober, lines in "The Yellow Wall-Paper": "a florid arabesque," "budding and sprouting in endless convolutions."

Regardless, it should now be clear that, despite the experimental nature of the subject matter, we find ourselves within the characteristic monotony of the psychedelic hallucination, the repeating pattern of the repeating pattern. This pattern is re-enacted yet again in Aldus Huxley's well-known 1953 publication, *Doors of Perception*—a book that not only mentions S. Weir Mitchell and Havelock Ellis as predecessors, and that proceeds to reenact, in Huxley's own recounting of his psychedelic experiences, the repeating pattern of the repeating pattern—but that has inspired countless subsequent psychedelic narratives, spiritual and speculative, popular and literary.

What is this repeating pattern of the repeating pattern, in which one's personal experience of intoxication—in other words, what practitioners of the narco-imaginary might conceptualize as "being-under-influence"—is communicated through the words of another, in which being-under-influence becomes writing-through-citation—and in which writing, as a prosthesis for being-under-influence, becomes citation-as-writing, a prosthetic prosthesis, supplement of the supplement. (Note that Silas Weir Mitchell, author of the earliest, most influential account of peyote intoxication, served as a surgeon during the Civil War; as a result of his interviews with patients whose limbs he had sawed off, Mitchell published groundbreaking studies documenting the phenomenon of the phantom limb.)

Perhaps we might consider the narco-imaginary as the phantom limb of the experimental subject; or, perhaps the narco-imaginary is a placebo effect, what one imagines the representation of drug use to be like; perhaps the narco-imaginary can be "like itself," but it can never "be itself"; perhaps what one calls the narco-imaginary is what one thinks one might call the narco-imaginary; perhaps the narco-imaginary is the experimental subject of the experimental subject of the experimental subject of the experimental subject of...

9

The experimental subject, the illusory figure through which so much of our knowledge of intoxication is written, encompasses a baffling, elliptical, oracular, seemingly impenetrable body of textual evidence. To understand what the experimental subject cannot fully articulate, the self-administered dose of the scientist confirms the narco-imaginary as a literary trope that intoxicates by insisting upon the vitality of what it cannot represent, the substance beyond language, that which it cannot quantify, the inimitable qualities of which elude linguistic capture, to which it must merely gesture through reference and repetition, citation and quotation.

"Obsessed and entranced, narcissistic, private, unable to achieve transference, the writer often resembles the addict," observes Avital Ronell. "Like the addict, such a writer is incapable of producing real value or stabilizing the truth of a real world."

Witness, for example, the efforts of Gordon Alles—and, subsequently, the heads of various pharmaceutical companies— seeking to exploit amphetamine, the compound Alles synthesized—first, by marketing the drug as an asthma remedy; then, as an antidote for depression; then, as a weight-loss medication; and so on, and so forth, until finally settling on the latest, most preferred use to date, a remedy for ADHD.

Sometimes you need a trick to get the song out of your head, even when it's a song you don't know, or can't remember. You have to get something on the page just to hear yourself think. Rose is a rose is a rose is a rose. A rose for Saint Jerry.

In my lap rests the notebook in which "Experiment" is written, followed by a colon. After the colon, the doctor's instructions: "keep a diary of your feelings; write about how you feel (every day, if possible); make entries for the next two weeks."

You've been given a protocol, you're the subject of your own experiment: take a dose, write about how you feel.

NOTES

78. The scene appears in James Szalapski's documentary, *Heartworn Highways* (1976).

VULTURES ARE WRITERS BY NATURE

The Butte Creek Mill & General Store lies along the old stage coach route that once linked the logging camps outside Butte Falls to the towns in Southern Oregon's Rogue Valley. Mt. McLoughlin rises beyond. The signs don't say so, but I like to think of this territory, from Mount McLoughlin, to Little Butte Creek, to the towns of Eagle Point and Medford, as Sam's land.

My memories of Sam adorn the repository of relics from my very earliest years of life. The stories I have been told by Janice—who was, and still is, my mother's dear friend, and who married Sam not long before I was born—have their place in my memory as if I had lived them. Janice tells me stories of a Ramsey that is me, but who I don't know. I have no memory of him but what I have been given, either by Janice, or by my parents, or by other friends and relatives.

I am told that Sam had almost no experience with children, and very little in the way of the usual demeanor that makes certain adults magnets for children. I am told that my affection for Sam—a toddler's affection, virtually inexplicable, perhaps an affection for the rough, work-worn textures of his clothes, or for his massive, dark beard, as much as his kind visage, or his personable demeanor—this affection was, for Sam, overwhelming.

There must be a well-worn phrase to describe the photographs featuring me and Sam together—the unabashedly beaming smile and gleeful radiance of the boy's face, alongside Sam's—"the very essence of joy," for example. The boy is, I am told, me—though he doesn't interest me as much as that phrase, "the very essence of joy." How the phrase invites us to acknowledge the real and true "essence of joy," otherwise known as sorrow. Or heartbreak. Or grief, or melancholy. Or, the truth, in vanishing—if that's what it is.

Whatever it is, in other words, that assumes permanence, as part of the realization that the people and the experiences that one most cherishes must someday come to an end—whatever it is that serves notice, as joy does, that the fact that one lives, matters—but only because, someday, one will not—and what's more, there have been others, already, whom one has loved, who already do not.

Sam died suddenly, unexpectedly, some weeks or days after the photographs were taken.

I am told that Sam loved the forest, that he was an enthusiastic outdoorsman, a fisherman and a man chock-full of local knowledge particular to Southern Oregon, that he knew of ancient Indian marketplaces, burial grounds, and archeological sites "discovered" by the so-called experts many years after his death; I am told that Sam and George, my father, worked together cutting, chopping, and selling firewood, and that it was Sam who passed along his passion for hunting morel mushrooms to my father; and I know that for many years after Sam's death,

George spent countless afternoons looking for morel mushrooms in the forest surrounding our house.

I imagine that George's hunt for mushrooms was not so much a hunt for mushrooms as it was a way of remembering Sam. I watched my father from afar—through a window, from across a field, an opening in the trees—and I remember that as I watched my father in his solitary pursuit of morel mushrooms, his face carried a weight no mushrooms could measure, a human weight, what some might describe as gravitas.

Gravitas is a word for other people's faces, it's not a word that one assigns to one's own. Many years after Sam's death, I was driving to the site of his memorial, a ranch we knew as Rancheria, and the memorial that held Sam's ashes was a pyramid built out of cement and river rocks and it had been capped with a white conical rock to mimic the symmetrical, iconic, volcanic silhouette of Mt. McLaughlin, rising just a day's hike into the distance.

I don't think that my brother, Aaron, was in "the van." George and Aaron found the van for me when I was in college, and when I had driven my first car, a '76 Chevy Nova, into the ground. The van was a baby blue '63 Chevy Econoline, with windows all around—the originals, intact—and George and Aaron had found the van for sale outside someone's house in Gold Hill, about an hour's drive from Butte Falls and Rancheria.

$800 was never better spent, but these are facts you don't need to know, even if I need to write them. What you need to know is that facts are like that well-spent $800: they sound like the measure of *something*, they carry the illusion of value when nothing else does.

Facts grow into something worth watering, even if the well is almost empty. They seem like something to know—but knowing facts does nothing to fix what you don't.

In any event, gravitas is not something I can claim to possess, even if it's something I might somehow "project." Gravitas arrives, or is somehow granted by events, or a given moment, or a certain context—or else it's not gravitas.

The original fence surrounding Sam's memorial finally caved in under the pressure of grazing livestock, who scratched themselves against the corner posts. I drove the van to Rancheria to help George repair Sam's memorial. I know that Quentin, Sam's son, was with me, and I remember that I affected a certain sobriety when I climbed into the van with Quentin; Aaron must have ridden in George's truck. I attempted gravitas, but I think it came off more like a hopelessly drunken man's imitation of sobriety.

Sam's funeral is one of my earliest memories. I remember that we sang songs together in the field where his memorial now stands—or rather, I listened to adults sing. I remember just one song, but I remember it so vividly, never to forget: "Will the Circle Be Unbroken." My sense is that the mystery of the lyrics struck me as having some weight, though at that time I had no means with which to measure:

> Will the circle be unbroken
> by and by, lord, by and by
> there's a better home awaiting
> in the sky, lord, in the sky

The sun and moon made circles in the sky—and turkey vultures, which you always saw circling high over Sam's land, and still do. But what did it mean—what does it mean—to "be unbroken"? Never to have been broken, or to have been fixed?

Quentin was going back to repair his father's memorial, and I was with him. I had no gravitas, even when I tried to wear it. Quentin wore a great big beard, like his father Sam, but Quentin's beard was red, whereas Sam's beard was black; Quentin had Sam's beard, in Janice's hair color—or Janice's hair color, in Sam's beard, or Sam had Sam's color, in Quentin's beard—my sobriety went missing in that beard, or maybe in Quentin's smile.

We smoked a joint on the way to Rancheria. I think Quentin wanted to steer the van for me while I lit it, because I was the one at the wheel, but I told him I didn't need help, and I was fumbling with the lighter, and it dropped under my feet somewhere. I picked it back up, reaching under my feet, one hand on the wheel. I remember the pedals, all the rubber gone, worn down to bare steel. How did I light a joint and drive the van, without power steering, up that winding dirt road to Rancheria, with log trucks careening around corners and Quentin making jokes and me, or what I remember as the me that some people must think of when they think of me—smoking pot and shifting and steering without looking at the road and affecting, what—gravitas?

Janice's eyes gleam and glisten with tears, even when she smiles. Her sparkle is Quentin's, too. What she means, even as a memory, is what Sam meant, which is something to read about—if somebody can write it—or something to write about, even if it can't be written.

It's the measure of something—sign of the hearth and heart, of where humanity is, or should be—card sent from where you should go, someday, if you can—where you should have been, already, or where you should go back to—if you can find a way to get back—wherever you are.

We used to pan for gold in Little Butte Creek, or maybe it was Sardine Creek. We liked to pretend that iron pyrite—fool's gold—was gold, proper. You can sink your teeth into Janice's sparkle, or Quentin's, it's pure gold. Your bite leaves a mark.

What is it that makes people so, I mean the finest people, the exceptionally human ones of us? What is it, this something they have, that you can't even find, except for odd occasions, you can't even remember what it's like, to be in the presence of whatever it is—

You can sink yourself into a narcotic stupor trying to define it, and wake up with a page full of something that takes wing and circles, as if there were no other purpose to anything, as if there were nothing else to do, ever, nothing whatsoever to do, but to take wing, and circle.

Turkey vultures are writers by nature. Not so much because they feed on the decaying flesh of the deceased, though it certainly doesn't disqualify them—but because their very existence depends upon that impulse to take wing and circle.

On more than one occasion, my father returned from his mushroom hunt talking not of the mushrooms he had found, and not of the mushrooms he had not found, but of Sam, and if not of Sam, of morel mushrooms, not of the finding and not of the not finding of morels, but of their curious habits, their tendency to appear in the same places, not year after year, but every other year, or every two or even every three years, or four, or five, so that one had to remember, one always needed to remember where one had found morels not last year, but the year before and the year before that; and if George returned from his morel hunt talking not of the curious habits of morel mushrooms, he might just as likely talk of the business of cutting firewood, or the business of selling firewood, and if not the firewood business, he might return from his morel hunt with some other story that directly or indirectly animated Sam's image.

After my divorce, I tried not to think, but I couldn't help it. I thought and thought, and nothing I thought meant anything, and the circles I made were just circles, and anything I tried to think brought me back to where I began, which was not where I wanted to be. I would spend what time I could with my children, and when my time with them was up, I would go nowhere, doing nothing. I tried to think of anything besides nothing, but I couldn't. Everything was nothing, and if it wasn't already nothing, well, anything could be. Anything would be, in fact—anything would be nothing, eventually.

One day I opened my mailbox, and inside I found a card, from Janice. "The children will be your light in the forest," Janice wrote.

The picture on the front of the card shows one of those historic buildings you see in Oregon's old logging towns, so long as they haven't burned or been bulldozed: wooden shingles, a Dutch gable or hip roof, a covered porch jutting out at the main entrance: "The Butte Creek Mill & General Store," the sign says.

I can't think of Janice, or Little Butte Creek, or Butte Falls, or forests, without thinking of Sam.

I sat down with Janice's card and let myself wander through Sam's land—except that I was living in New York City, and so to get to Sam's land, I had to forge my way, through memory and back, to what memories I had made out of other peoples' stories.

Sometimes I was Ramsey, in Sam's lap, and sometimes, I was Sam; but when I was Sam, it wasn't Ramsey in Sam's lap. Sam's lap became Ramsey's lap, and it was one or both of my own sons sitting in that lap.

Click and the camera flashes.

I like to think that forests will forever be those groves through which Sam's image passes when, as light softens and fog drifts across low-slung branches to settle amidst thick trunks, the persistent drip from drenched branches is the only sound, save the crunch of twigs underfoot.

I also like to think that Sam possessed a kind of ancient knowledge possessed by those who live in forests and those who hunt morels, a knowledge of slow time and a knowledge of habits not our own, and habits not of some other animal, not domestic habits, and not habits yielded by some careful breeding process manufactured by humans, but the habits of some species altogether different, altogether fungal.

MY DOING

I don't want to write about digging in a profound way, I don't want to remember why I started digging or what purpose it served, I don't want to allegorize every damn act, I only want to say that I dug a hole and spent a day doing it and at the end there was a hole in the ground, a few feet deep, not very round, with roots and rocks reaching out toward its center. I made this hole with a shovel and a pick and I remember that when I started digging there were a number of difficulties. Tree roots obtrude, after a single layer of decaying leaves and black soil the clay is orange and firm, almost impenetrable, and sometimes there are rocks buried beneath the clay. The difficulty with rocks is that when you strike a rock with a shovel or a pick you can't tell whether it's a small rock or a big rock, you hear a noise when you strike a rock, and then you see a rock or a piece of a rock and until you've fully dislodged the entire animal you can't be certain just how big it might be. When I dug my hole in the ground I wasn't very old, I was maybe eight or nine, I had an idea to dig a hole and I took the shovel which was really a shovel, though someone else might call it a spade, a spade is an elegant word and I remember that what I had in my hands was really a wooden-handled shovel, rusty at the blade and worn at the places on the handle where hands had most often gripped it. I also remember that we had any number of shovels around our house, some for my mother to use in her garden, and these looked like a shovel ought to look, and others my father used for construction work, and these shovels were flat-nosed shovels, and then there were shovels for digging fencepost holes, and these shovels had two handles and a hinge in the middle, and two blades, and when you used this kind of shovel you had to pull it apart and thrust it into the earth and then push it together to lift the dirt out of the ground, and then there was a long, narrow shovel that my father actually called a spade, and there was yet another kind of shovel which was wide and flat and this shovel was for snow. Once, at the Grange Co-Op, which was a store that sold seeds and hoses and many other items and implements my mother used in her garden, I saw a whole row of shovels, all kinds of shapes and sizes, and I remember that I was surprised to see that some shovels had blades painted green, and some were painted red, and I remember wondering why our shovels weren't green or red, until I realized that at one time our shovels had been green or red, but the paint had worn away and what was left was only a rusty blade and no trace of paint. One of these shovels, perhaps the one that I used to dig my hole, I used for a Halloween costume when I was little, or at least littler than I was when I dug my hole, and so when I dug my hole I may have remembered my Halloween costume as one memory I had of a shovel. I was a prospector that Halloween, and to be a prospector there were a few things that you needed. One thing was a hat, which was not a cowboy hat but a beat-up type of hat with a round-ish, malleable brim, so that it looked dented here and there, and you also needed a red bandana, and a beard or something that looked more or less beard-like, and a flannel shirt, and blue jeans tucked into boots of some kind that came to just below the knees, and finally you needed a pan, because prospectors used pans, or if your parents wouldn't let you carry their pans around you needed a shovel, because without a shovel someone might mistake you for a hobo, and you weren't a hobo, you were a prospector. But when I dug my hole I was no prospector, I just dug, and I had an idea that I would do just that, dig, and when I was done there would be a hole. What I did not know when I dug this hole was that there would be a time, a later time, when digging the hole would be a memory, and the memory would be of a time when I would do some things just to do them, for no other reason than that, to do, as something to do and have done; and so I can say that, whereas at one time I would dig a hole for no other reason than to dig a hole, now if I were to dig a hole for no reason, others might say my digging must mean something, must be a sign of something I might otherwise be unable or unwilling to express, whereas I might think that I was only nostalgic for a time when I would do things just to do them and for no other reason than that.